NEW *&* SELECTED POEMS

Also by James J. McAuley:

Observations, Mt. Salus Press, Dublin, 1960
A New Address, Dolmen Press, Dublin, 1965
The Revolution, verse satire, Lantern Theatre, Dublin, 1966
Draft Balance Sheet, Dolmen Press, Dublin, 1970
The Exile's Recurring Nightmare, San Francisco, 1974
After The Blizzard, Univ. of Missouri Press, Colombia MO, 1975
Praise!, libretto, composer Wendal Jones. Spokane Symphony
        Orchestra, Chorus, and Tenor Solo, 1981
Recital, Dolmen Press, Dublin, 1982
The Exile's Book Of Hours, Confluence Press, Idaho, 1982
Coming & Going: New & Selected Poems, Univ. of Arkansas Press,
Fayetteville, AR, 1989
Meditations, With Distractions: Poems 1988-98, Univ. of Arkansas
Press, Fayetteville, AR, 2001

NEW & SELECTED POEMS

JAMES J. McAULEY

Foreword by Paula Meehan

DEDALUS PRESS

First published in 2005 by
The Dedalus Press
13 Moyclare Road
Baldoyle
Dublin D13 K1C2
Ireland

Reissued in 2023.

www.dedaluspress.com

ISBN 978-1-904556-34-3 (paperback)
ISBN 978-1-904556-35-0 (hardback)

Dedalus Press titles are available in Ireland
from Argosy Books (www.argosybooks.ie) and in the UK
from Inpress Books (www.inpressbooks.co.uk)

Cover image: 'Full Moon' by Paula Meehan.

The Dedalus Press receives financial assistance from
The Arts Council / An Chomhairle Ealaíon.

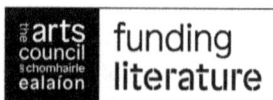

for the family

ACKNOWLEDGEMENTS

Grateful acknowledgement is made to University of Arkansas Press who have granted permission to include poems in this selection from *Coming & Going, New & Selected Poems,* and *Meditations, with Distractions*; and to Colin Smythe for permission to include poems from *Recital* (Dolmen, 1982).

Versions of some of these poems (1998-2004) have previously appeared in periodicals and anthologies, to the editors of which we are grateful: *Image, Poetry Northwest, Writers' Forum, Poetry Ireland Review, Cyphers, The SHOp, Southword, The Living Stream,* Festschrift for Theo Dorgan, ed. Niamh Morris, 2002, *Out to Lunch,* ed. John McNamee, for the Barretstown Gang Camp, Bank of Ireland Arts Centre/Poetry Ireland, 2002, *Forgotten Light,* anthology ed. Louise C. Callaghan, for the Alzheimer's Foundation, 2003.

Contents

from *Meditations with Distractions* (2001)

FOREWORD
Paula Meehan

⇒

This is an auspicious book. It is the first book published by the newly incarnated Dedalus Press, as it passes from the hands of its founder John F. Deane into the hands of Pat Boran, its new editor and director. Synchronicitously, as Pat is a native of County Laois, it was that great Laois publisher and book maker Liam Miller who was responsible for Jim McAuley's last Irish outing. *Recital*, in 1982 was one of the last, if not the last, of the Dolmen Press titles. *Recital* got lost literally and epistemologically in the confusions attendant on the end of Dolmen.

This looping back into the contemporary Irish poetry pool reflects a looping back in Jim McAuley's life—he retired from Eastern Washington University, in the north-west of the United States in 1998, and moved back to Ireland, to a house in Ballyknockan looking down over Blessington lake. It's tempting, given the stoneworking traditions of Ballyknockan, where even humble cottages are lintelled and silled with exquisitely chiselled granite, to see Jim in his retirement (so called), hurling his granite slabs of poetry down on the sodthem and begorrah that is the new Ireland. Wicklow, the Garden of Ireland, being now the Illegal Waste Dumping Capital of Ireland, Jim brings the returnee's clear-eyed gaze to both its beauty and its treachery. If he sings the garden into being, it is the garden as is.

When Jim left Ireland in 1966, by boat from Galway for New York, he was heading into the real sixties—remembering that the sixties didn't actually start in Ireland until the seventies. He was ripped untimely from the bars off Grafton Street, sodden miasmas of the fifties really, remembering also that the fifties didn't end in Ireland until the seventies.

Jim was heading for the University of Arkansas, at Fayetteville, in the deep south, to the writing programme directed by James Whitehead, for graduate studies that would lead to a Master of Fine Arts in Poetry. This was the new model —poetry passed on by a generation of poets who had come into the universities as teachers, where they enjoyed, or quite often suffered, a complex relationship with the traditional English Departments. The new model was workshop based, it was practicum, it was a major departure in the ethos of how literature lives in the academy. The English Departments would continue teaching the theory of literature but there was often this tribe of actual writers, poets and storytellers, many of them availing of the G.I. Bill's education promise, holing up in the Creative Writing Departments making poems and stories and not shy about intervening in the neat extrapolation of the theorists. An ecosystem was developing within the groves that has had, and continues to have, profound implications for the way poetry is passed on. The trans-mission. There and here. (How many Irish Universities in the last few years have started offering degrees in Creative Writing?)

To rattle James Joyce for a moment Jim was forging in the smithy of his conscience his own soul. Civil rights, Vietnam, Bob Dylan, Women's Liberation, Black Power, Gay Rights, Flower Power, Acid, the bus Further. It is the age of Jimi Hendrix, the Seattle Orpheus soothing the stirred beast with The Star Spangled Banner, but not like they play it in Kansas, Dorothy.

Jim plunged into these waters and was swept in the currents where the street meets the school, where the quest for personal liberation meets the military-capitalist-political-machine. The powerful demotic force that is English as she is spoke in the US meets the sophisticated, classically educated, Jesuit formed, Irish poet with his pure lyric, his ancient music, its plumbline into the bronze age, its plumbline back to Amergin, and his well thumbed English masters from 'Wyatt to Robert Browning, to Father Hopkins in his crowded grave'.

When he was headhunted (or rescued from destitution) in 1970 to establish and direct the Creative Writing Programme at Eastern Washington University in Spokane, he made for the great north west. And there he set up home for nearly thirty years. What did he meet there in the land of Roethke, Hugo, Stafford, Snyder, Kizer, Kesey, and le Guin?

He met the Spokane Indians: People of the deer and salmon. It must have been like looking directly into the bronze age mind of our own island. The Spokane Indians had still lived in their bronze age up to only a couple of hundred years ago. The lineaments of the ancient order were plain to see even through the prism of the reservation. His native American students were teaching him a new pastoral. He was even made an associate of AIM.

And then just down the road there was Fairchild Airforce Base, number two on the Russian nuclear target list. And Hanford nuclear town where the bombs were built. And oh the majesty of the Cascade mountain range, with Mt. Hood, Mt. Adams, Mt. Rainier, and Mt. St. Helen's, Loowit—the Smoky One, the volcano who would blow her top at 8.32 am on the 18th of May 1980.

The bear and the elk still roamed the old-growth forest. These forces, these energies, these 'animals as persons' are present to the poems. Floods, blizzards, nature red in tooth and claw. And Jim starts calling on the Great Spirit coterminously now with God the Father. His theology is shifting. His students are shaking him up. His classes are filled with eco-feminists, farm boys and girls from the wheatfields (the rich Palouse fertility), indigenous people, supporters of Reagan's moral majority juxtaposed with anti-nuclear activists. The Idaho branch of the Ku Klux Klan are given permission to hold a meeting in the university. The administration was right wing and Jim is ferociously democratic, ferociously just. How did he stick it?

His best teaching years—sober, sane, with his beloved Deirdre and his last son Daniel; open house, open heart for his students. Meticulous craftsman. Powerful maker and wielder of a line. But letting us find our own way home *appassionato*.

He revived EWU Press, a kind of semi-defunct entity within the university that had been used to publish occasional faculty work. He turned the press into a vital presence, publishing such poets as Carolyn Kizer, Diana O'Hehir, Thomas Reiter, Gabriela Mistral in translation by Christiane Jacox Kyle, Elizabeth Cook-Lynn, and Sam Green.

And since 1978, initially in the Burren for its first two years, and subsequently in Dublin, he constituted the Eastern Washington University's Summer Writing Workshops, intensive seminars where tyropoets and story makers from both sides of the Atlantic and indeed beyond, would gather to be taught by Jim and a pool of Irish writers that was a roll call of the best in contemporary Irish poetry and fiction. He secured scholarship money for Irish participants, often young writers making their first connections to peers and teachers. The reading series associated with these workshops constituted a high quality festival at the heart of summer, in the heart of Dublin.

All this service to the muse of others and the chronicling of it, for Jim's life has been above all one of service to the gifts of others, must not be allowed overshadow the true auspicious nature of this Selected and New Poems. We can chart the arc of a poet who is amongst the most formally ambitious of his contemporaries and yet who can surrender in the face of the power of expressionism — to the point where formal and organic verse no longer have to be oppositional, as some of the feebler theorists would have us believe. Descendant of the scribe and hedgeschoolmaster Michael Óg O Longáin, he has something of the hedgeschoolmaster about him still. A sure belief, maybe, that learning, and he is a seriously learned man, like poetry, can not be commodified.

I mentioned at the beginning that this book was a looping back into the Irish tradition. At last we can see the full and magnificent heft of the poetry. A missing chapter can be written in the annals; a voice can be heard, now singing chorus, now singing solo. We are so much the richer for it. As Mandelshtam has it, 'The lovely pattern cannot be wiped out.'

Old friend, bird seer, teacher of the craft, midwife to babypoets, champion of the broken, our humanist master in whose light we write, I am honoured to fore-word thee.

New Poems
1998-2004

Pastorale
Homage to John Clare

One sheep mocks another, laughing nervously.
They steal each other's ground but don't seem to move.
The Great White Bull of Ballyknockan complains
In a loud moan from the steep field, an old mad monarch
Though he wears the slave's nose-ring and chain. The cows
Attend him with sly obeisance, munching, keeping
Their troubles to themselves. Sleek couples from the local
Rookery flap uphill to swing on the powerline and gossip
In their hoarse *patois*: "Those damn magpies,
Those damn cats, that tractor..." As one they break off
And put the air to the test, climbing the gust
They picked up on its way from hill to lake. Erratic
Bedlam maniacs, they sail over the bungalows, drop
Like revelling bandits into their beechtree camp.

The chaffinches shift on their perches, uneasy.
Then the swaying sapling branches propel them one
After another into the bare thornbush with the wrinkled
Half-rotten berries they know will get them drunk.
They eat their fill. Sobersides robin delivers
A shrill homily—"Finches! Have you no homes...?"
They bully him out of his usual thorny pulpit
To a larch-tip at the forest edge. From there
A herd of deer has made a path up the misty hill
Into the ravens' domain, through spruce,
Furze, bramble, rockfall, reedy rivulets.

Flight

When swans lift from the lake's
Broken mirror, envy
Unsteadies us. Silently,
Clouds climb from the world's edge
Over us, shape-changing, and fear
Empties our bellies. Priest,
In your cape of white feathers, lift
Your holy wings over us, coax
The sky-spirit to save us
By the powers of the swan,
The swallow, the lark, the dove.

&

Daedalus, genius of labyrinths,
Who warned your son against pride,
Teach us grief. Where on Icaria
Can we find the temple you built
For the wings you offered Apollo
When the sea-god claimed your boy?

&

At Rouen, Rheims, Chartres, death
Is a joke, a bat-winged crone
Carved high on a wall. On sky-
Blue glass, frail-winged angels
Pass between heaven and earth.
So be it. We will kneel here.

&

Machines to take man's measure:
Leonardo's device, an abstruse
Horizontal windmill, geared
For a soldier on a battlefield
To conquer gravity
Before we knew its laws.

Look! Look! The balloon!
So high above the doomed court
That the brothers in their flying
Gondola can't be seen.
Look now: from *that* balloon
An artillery officer
Is directing Napoleon's guns.
Arma virumque cano.

From waterwheel to steam
Engine is hardly a mile
Downriver. The roar and clatter
Can change shepherds into oafs
Begging in the towns. Bring
Men with pen and paper:
We will sign for the air we breathe.

&

Ὀλοκαυνον: for Hitler's war
My father ferried diplomats,
Clergymen, spies of all kinds,
Between Dublin and Bristol
In a neutral passenger plane.

He dropped no bombs, shot
No one down. Then an old
Bomber converted for cargo
Gave him his Viking funeral
On take-off from Tehran,
To fulfil irony's law.

వ

Victory! Jet-plane and rocket-bomb
Excited the entrepreneurs
When the New World Empire rose
From the flames of Stalingrad,
Dresden, Hiroshima, Nagasaki,
Destroyed in order to save them
According to the ancient rites
Of *Dulce et Decorum*.
To die for Oil and Steel,
We need only wait in our houses.

వ

Through the outrageous heat
The firemen climbed past us
To their mortal duty.
Fumes tore the air from our lungs—
Liquid flame poured down on us—
When there was no other place
We stretched out our arms on the blue
Space between earth and heaven,
Calling, "We love you. We love you."

Approach
for Kay Powers

I approach while you cry quietly at the end
Of your day's teaching, what you call The Shift.
A tough week. A kid shot dead, others who lift
Their own weight in sorrow, others who send
Their little notes round the class, feeling this
Must be a TV show. Slouched at their desks,
Hard rock to work loose, they wear the masks
Of fallen angels glaring at the abyss.

How would you give stone life? Your tears well
From that dizzy pit of grief, catch in the throat
When they've gone trooping off at the bell
Like nymphs and shepherds who follow the god-goat
Dancing to hell, and so afraid of hell.
Come on, pick up your stuff, I'll walk you out.

The Hill Walkers
for Michael

We would climb one shoulder only to find
Another slope ahead of us. It seemed
There was no summit. Mist hung in shreds
Over moorland and blurred the sky's outline
Where in clear weather the mountain should
Be answering to the map we studied.

We paused at a well-spring, a brown
Quagmire really, that filled an oval
Basin below a granite outcrop
Called by locals "*An Tobar Géar.*"
They gave no saint's name to bitter water,
Nor powers to a place so lost to grace.

Tom, no saint himself, called us over
With an oath. He squatted awkwardly
Before a plant that rose two feet or more
Below him from a tuft of reeds
Rustling stiffly at the edge. I paid
Little heed: a bullrush or iris

Could survive this boggy height. But Tom
Called again. The stem, straight and fibrous,
Jointed where a single leaf raised
A stiff metallic yellow blade, tapered up
To a spire of tightly-knit violet buds,
As long as my hand from wrist to fingertip.

Christy, the botanist—or as close to one as any
Who'd keep our company—was puzzled.
He bent out over it, as near as he dared;
Straightened, and turned away. He was unsure,
But thought it a poisonous garlic. He'd seen
A plant like it in the Botanical Gardens.

Its lurid flower nodded when the wind
Stole down the mountain to stroke it.
Richard, our "silent partner," grasped it,
His foot on the tuft it grew from,
And wrenched it out.

A knot of roots, a Gorgon's head, bulged
From its crusted base. The disturbed mud
Stank, like sulphur. Richard dropped it back
Without a word. We watched it keel over.
Its thin, sinewy arm with its violet hand
Drooped slowly into the slime and sank.

The Snipe
for Michael Davitt
(King Lear, Act III, Sc. 2)

Prologue
I started a snipe from the heather
On the shoulder of Moanbane.
It skittered and skimmed downhill,
Low over the bog, its heathery form
Woven into the air by the white
Flash of its underwing. I sighted,
Led it over a furze-bush, fired
Quickly. It veered, dropped
The left wing, and dived behind
A sandy granite boulder. I followed it
Downhill, with questions in my head.

I
It wasn't hunger. A bag-full of them, hung,
Gutted, plucked, and cooked ten days from now
Would scarcely make a meal for a penitent
On *Sceilg Mhichíl.* Nor was it anger. What
Anger would follow me up from the house
Across rock-strewn pasture, the fern-choked ditch,
Into the sapling larch and spruce—spires
For the chapels of tough furze—onto the bog?
What rage could feed on bog-cotton, reeds,
The tinny clatter of a nameless stream, the hiss
Of wind in heather? I fired into its veering flight,
I saw it drop behind that boulder, and followed it
Downhill, confusion in my head.

II

Nor was the gun a surrogate, a denial or need
Out of loneliness, though I lived long enough,
God knows, in that empty house, its dust-mote
Silences. And as for guilt: gunshot, well-aimed
Or not, either rips through the unforgiven or
Whistles at innocence and changes nothing.
This canvas bag, designed to bring home game,
More often carries stones with curious shapes
From a beach, or a piece of sodden bog-oak
To be dried, carved, polished and set up
As a charm against false pride, false accusation.

III

Was I tired? Yes. I admit it. World-weary.
Wouldn't it be fine if these arguments
Between Self and Soul could be scattered
Like bird-shot and blown by the four winds
Over the squelching bog? Am I looking
For peace, like poor old Lear on his heath?

Flash of the snipe's underwing—gun-blast—all
Moanbane's gossiping elements tune their fiddles
And pipes, but can make no tune
To animate resentment's frozen mask.

Epilogue
I rounded the boulder where
I saw the snipe drop. No sign.
The rising wind coursed along
Moanbane's flank. Twelve paces
Beyond the rock I saw one wing
Twitching in the heather.
I lifted it by this wing,
The jet eyes clouded, five coins
Of blood on the matted feathers.
I buried it where it fell.

A Last Cigarette
for Theo Dorgan

Before the steps to the Dart,
stop a second. The State
Of Grace presents itself
Displayed in the cobwebbed
Window of a derelict
Shop that still offers Wills'
Woodbines to leathery salts
Off the docks, a few
Coffin-nail puffs down
The cobbled lane where

The new breed of power suits
Designer ties and shoes
That make statements and eyes
That glitter with dark
Agendas push through the stiles
Thinking they have to stave
In a few ribs to get a feel for
The thing it takes to make
A living these times—
So many, who would have thought
Or cared to think at all
Between their headsets?

Three slow breaths
Settle the mind down.
A waste of breath, really,
The wait to catch his
Breath on the footbridge
After the short steep climb.
The glass walls keep

The weather where he'd want it,
So he can idle while
The rushed street creatures
Head north and south, home or
Hell, bet each way…. Back down
At their level he'd have to breathe
Whatever they have
By way of a fair wind.

Wheels rasp on rails
That can't take them away
From the trite tunes that sell
Aspirin and trips

To Malaga. Get that
Whiff of ordure off the strand?
Nothing to worry about,
Since it won't compute
With the numbers that tick
On the screens all the way
From the glassy corporate
Fortresses across the river.

Neck-hairs stand alert
When the man in the greasy mack
Pushes past to get off
At the stop before his.
Hardly a menace, yet
Reminiscent of hard times.

He turns and arranges the pillow
Under his ear, which seethes with
The tempo of blood thudding
The arteries at more or less
The sea's pulse-rate. Soon, he's asleep.

The Damascus Epiphany

"Ratcatcher" Savannah's criminal mind
Taught him to look criminal: his mane
Of greasy white hair streaked grey; the beard
Exaggerating his triangular face;
Eyes brittle black in bony sockets. Thin
And small as a twelve-year-old; shoulders clamped
In a shrug, perpetually defending against blows.

A cruel nickname, yet it connected him
To old wives' tales. The State had licensed him
To counsel neurotics, reveal them to themselves,
Start them on a programme of bliss....
His specialty? Those divas of beauty parlours,
Fitness rooms, discreet lounges.

Savannah, his adoptive family's name,
Gave a useful exotic touch to his practice.
He affected a half-whisper which he seemed
To think disarming, a devious hiss, as if air
Leaked from his ears through the thick hair
That concealed them while he uttered questions,
Innuendos: "These feelings, now, when did you first...?"

Never "Why?" No interest in motive, only
The chain of psychic events his patient was digging
Out for him, this rosy blonde, from when her cousin
Deflowered her at fifteen, to the weekend liaisons,
To marriage and divorce. Now he leant forward
So she would see he was smiling, his thin mouth
A knowing rictus, sharing his success with her,

This breakthrough to a fragile present!
The fat bookshelf Buddha was also smiling,
A clue to Savannah's version of the real.
Spring, '63: a frizzy-haired student he had loved
Convinced him to bring her to a talk
On meditation. Twice a week he squatted
On a rug, lost in contemplation of his beloved
Flower-child's half-lotus. But when they flew
To India she found her guru, who took her
Like a meal of figs. The guru laughed
At Savannah's anger and urged him toward
Enlightenment. He left the ashram
To the wiry Indians, the hophead Yanks,
The screaming English schoolgirls.

❧

Between Delhi and London he discovered himself
Stranded on the MEA Comet at Damascus airport.
Soldiers strolled through the cabin. He kept quiet
When they frogmarched the man behind him
From the plane. The passengers raised a hubbub.
Troops on the terminal roof were training their guns
Right at his window—he was *sure*! After the sun crashed
In flames on the desert, floodlights trapped the plane
In their merciless glare. Near midnight, hoarse
Loudspeakers revealed shocking secrets in Arabic
For all to hear. At last, no warning, the engines
Throttled up; the plane slid away from the lights,
Turned round and picked up speed along the runway.
Then they were climbing angelically
Through the brilliant stars.

The age of Aquarius was over for him. Half-asleep
In the darkened cabin, he knew, *he knew!* That voice
From the airport speakers, those monotone labials,
Released his soul for renewal as a healer of souls.
Now, thirty years on, a pirate of the psyche,
He leans from behind her and traces her lips
With his thumb, his other hand cupping her breast.
"You see?" He whispers, "You're free! Let go
These old fears!" She startles like a wounded
Leveret. He withdraws his hands and sidles
To hold the door open, head lodged between
The crooked shoulders. His onyx smile fixes her
As she passes to find her new cage
And snap it shut on herself.

Iris

Not how you would be thought of, your colour
Being grey, silky, like a second skin, your hair
Flecked with it. Now, hearing your way of saying
Iridescent while I read your poem, three years
After your death, I am compelled to check
You out in Ovid, Lamprière, Bulfin, then
A book of flowers, where I discover you
On marshy ground, not grey exactly—in fact
A pretty blue-grey, a quiet type, with a green cowl
To shelter the thoughtful inclined head.

Not at all the bright-winged messenger
Who'd drown the world if Juno put you up to it,
But a quiet sylph, who could colour her message
With a sly tilt of the head, those grey eyes steady,
Lips pursed, making a pretence of kissing.

You could supply so many ambiguities—
Gradations and streaks and tones of grey and blue—
That for twenty years I saw your story told
Where the sky lay on the wintry hills, weighed down
With tears Mnemosyne allows for you:
Flower, messenger, poet.

Lost At Sea

That old woman has just walked past the bus stop
And stopped to look over a garden wall, leaning
Forward, almost on tip-toe. She had that old
Dream again: gaslight, tram-bells clanging,
Her man Jack paying her a visit. *When we've cleared*
Port, that's when the wind picks up, that's when
The skipper sends the word to make all fast,
Pay out the lifelines. That's how she was widowed,
Jack swept overboard making ropes fast in a storm.
When she peers over the wall she feels she's relating,
In her own odd way, an account of herself
To her dead able-seaman on her way home.

She's been to the harbour again, can't help herself,
Just to look out past the lighthouse where he went missing.
She's wearing her sky-blue Queen-Mother outfit as usual,
Her nineteen-forties perm, the black patent-leather handbag
She bought for going to that Technical School
Where she learned typing and book-keeping so,
After you got yourself killed, careless bugger, she could
Get work that paid enough to keep her house,
The widow's pension too little for comfort....

Was that her cat? Far from home, for him. But no,
Not his black-and-white face. Like a wee clown-face, his.
Waits on no man when that phone goes off so loud
Because she won't wear a hearing-aid. This used to be
Old Nell's home. Glasshouse at the back for tomatoes
And delicate flowers and starting lettuce to plant out later.
Nothing fancy though, too much trouble. God rest her.
Sold off for next to nothing after all her care.

And here's God still in her head, still nagging her
To Sunday Service, after she got rid of Him forever
When Jack went missing. The old woman
In the sky-blue Queen-Mother frock-coat,
Who knew none of the new neighbours, looked back
Along the street and turned abruptly. She was getting
More forgetful, she told herself, and laughed aloud.

The Holy Wars

At Shannon the troops are uniformed as clowns
For their big act in the desert, so they'll appear
To disappear in a mirage as they steal up
On the enemy, whose uniforms are scarves
And robes, as for a Gothic Mystery play.
Both sides bought their arms from the same suppliers.

The first few wars took centuries, played out on foot
And horseback, with arrows, spears, lots of gold.
Christ and Mohammed were the heavenly generals
Whose names alone could make the blood burst
From enemy eye-sockets, and enemy citadels
Roar and roast in pitiless hell-flames.

Arnold observed the tides of Faith recede,
Split into factions, and another turbulent age
Set heretic and cleric at each other. Both
Dressed in black sackcloth, and each
Bound the other to rack and stake, burned sin
Out of city and hamlet, palace and cathedral.
But you know all this, don't you? You've read your histories.

Or do you still construe the seers' scribblings,
So you can keep the apocalyptic horsemen
Steadily in touch with the ages of stone,
Iron, bronze, gold, steel, plutonium?
Do you still find a grand design, a godsent
Saving plan for the mosque, temple, church,
So rabbi or imam or bishop can acclaim
Rulers to be obeyed, enemies to be crushed?

War on every page, rumours in every café,
Revolution whenever the army sides with the poor,
Those staring skulls demanding release from life.
And the bankers still hide the hoards of the nameless few
Behind their simpering, their colonnaded bunkers.
All this has been common knowledge since the trading
In oils and unguents and holy relics, the Hanseatics….

Every age has had its fifth columns, its pigeon post,
Its tranquillisers, its 'credible evidence', whatever
Gratifies the Church Militant, the Superego,
Whatever soothes the savage breast in its bomber jacket,
The clown whose family friends, just for a joke,
Gave him the Constitution to play with, let him declare
A "crusade" against terror while they were arranging
To use the army again as a marketing tool,
Free up the oil supplies, show off new weaponry,
Agitate the hornets' nests of Islam,
And stimulate product demand, worldwide.

Meanwhile, in Another Part of the War

On the street of the concrete refugee tenements
That have collapsed into the smoking holes
The Israeli rockets blew open at dawn's early light,
The sundered limbs and torsos of a Jenin family
Lie with the shards and dust of their household,
Three generations, shredded like paper dolls.

There are no heads to be found. They never had heads.
If they had heads, the Israeli spokesman assures
The State Department, the U.N., the Believers,
The CNN camera, with his shy smile, in
His Noo Yock twang, they wouldn't have been
Where the terrorists were.

        "Of the three-month-old infant,
"Crushed in its cradle, and the eighty-year-old
"Shepherd who retired twenty years ago when Israelis
"From Russia drove off his flock at gunpoint,
"And his son's wife, and the schoolboy, all buried
"In the holes the rockets made, which ones
"Were the terrorists?" A voice off-camera asks.

But the spokesman shrugs and smiles
Shyly. The cameras and the microphones
Are already turned off.

        There were survivors. One, some say
The mother of two victims, has volunteered
To take the bus to Jerusalem.

Ambiguity

The man who came to his rooms with a history
Of ulcers told the doctor a story, hardly new,
Yet bemusing enough to record it in his memoirs.
Even after his death, this curious anti-hero refused
To let go his grip on the doctor's conscience; a grain
Of sand under the eyelid.
                Stocky; metal-grey hair,
Well-worn wool jacket, navy trousers, the sort
The country's police wore then....In obvious pain
From the duodenum, the whole body tensed
In the effort to conceal his condition. From whom?
Forty-three, though his clenched jaw and rigid sinews
Put another twenty years on him.
                   Besotted with anxieties
That nothing but death itself could wrench from him,
His head sank to the pillow, resigned
To the stethoscope, thermometer, the doctor's fingers
Probing until they found pain's hair-trigger.
                  Under anaesthetic he began to confess
To crimes that, had he committed them, would howl
Their nature through town and country: three children
Burned in a fire; a whole family destroyed
On the border when their car somersaulted;
That night of shame with the maddened widow and
The murdered corpse upstairs.
              The doctor assumed the drug elicited
This narrative, though he remembered how
These crimes had obsessed the whole country for months.

He drained the syringe of morphine into the vein.
Little to be done: peritonitis.
                Soon, the blood-taste
Would rise in his mouth, the taste of perpetual anger.

Sixteen Nocturnes

These pieces were first written into a lined copybook with an italic fountain pen, over a period of about six weeks in the autumn of 2003, late at night, just before sleep, so I've called them "nocturnes," though what they have in common with musical nocturnes is incidental. The "voices" are varied, not necessarily my own, with varied degrees of reliability....

I

A moment: the longest time we can stay
Absolutely still; the interval between
Diastole and systole, before we must
Continue our *momentum,* the rush
Of blood that chases thought, the ice-cliff
Poised over the insistent swell of ocean.

II

Great Spirit, whose voice the wind drives down
Between the hills, whose flocks of sheep and rooks
Answer your praise for them and their kind,
White and black, bleat and caw—how can they hear
What we dare not? Is truth what we cannot understand
In that sibilant breathing of the lakeside pines?

Is it praise they hear, heron alert at the brook's mouth,
Fox taking step for step along the thorn hedge?
Isn't it just fancy that these creatures enjoy
Your favours more than we?
You keep from us only your understanding:
Without it, we must accept all we hear in the wind,
As the obdurate Ballyknockan stones accept.

III

This silly, dangerous lane! I want to see how far
I can follow it across its banal corrugations
On the way to seeing my homeland in a new way
So I may, so to say, introduce myself to her,
And perhaps persuade a little nourishment from her
For the journey, which will take me, I believe,
Over the massif and into that benign valley of the saintly
Whose séances first awoke in my deepest instincts
The will to seek the paths, untrodden since
Blacksmith, stonemason, and three-card-trickster
No longer trek there to pray and reflect. Nevertheless,
These journeys lead us toward the light, after
The arduous climb when we cross the last hill-shoulder
And descend beside the cascade rattling in its rocks
And hissing fitfully into the glen, and we reach the bank
Of the upper lake and look south with the sun at zenith.
The light has taken the substance of water there
For its own element. These mirages are why
We have travelled here, to understand what the saint
Perceived that found him a home here, only to be
Overtaken by other pilgrims of the light who followed
The river through its valley, searching.

IV

A little-known piece by Dvořák
Traumerei or *Canzone,* I imagined,
For the sake of the words' exciting sounds.
Echoes and vibrations and fugitive thoughts
Scurried among the rising/falling passages
Between pianoforte and violin, viola
And cello, another clement air scarcely heard,
Intake of breath, score-page quickly turned
In the pauses. So much was rendered simply
Because the instruments themselves evoked
Memory, sympathy, in such sharp detail:

Languid fireside loving, a mantelpiece figurine
From Japan, exotic foliage in the Kashan rug—
All weighted by the pattern twined in the sound
Suspended in recalled affection, recalled sorrow.

V

Past eleven, two nights before the solstice,
And the lake is still reluctantly accepting
The sky's light. Below in Carrigacurra
A dog barks frantically. Then it's so quiet,
The air so still between two weathers,
That the mind's work, thought itself, rests
Between light on water and light on cloud.

VI

Ah! Trumpets! A great man for the brass, Bruckner,
Wouldn't you say? Something *ur-Gothique*
About those spiky crescendos he builds in the Fourth
Symphony, I've always thought. Of course, not every
Conductor might interpret the score that way,
And loan the brasses so much muscle from beginning
To end. But you, no doubt, are here on another
Matter, yes? Love? Death? Taxes? Yes?

VII

That actor was also in the play we saw
That reminded me of Beckett's *Molloy,* played
As an Ulster peasant. Last night he had four
Encores for the ballad he sang in the last act,
Tone-deaf, deadpan, a dirge from a crypt.
Then, "Git along wit ye now," called offstage.
You weren't sure—were you?—whether he was still
Acting, or driven mad by the role he had to play,
And he a noble chap, by all accounts,
Many notable performances, accolades, standing
Ovations. His true glory, though, will come from what

He'll make of the after-life, how he'll play his role then
And there. He'll chasten us, I'll wager. We'll see him, yes,
As a wild, wily saint, the only role he's fit for.

VIII

Never mind: the train of thought gets stuck
At times, in a station on its way to the terminus.
But its one remaining passenger isn't too bothered,
All the time he needs, he thinks, to solve the puzzle;
Plenty of time to assess the *gaucherie* of his colleague
Matthew, who would correct the younger John
On matters of no importance, details in the report
Which wouldn't have changed the outcome in
Seven generations. *This*, he thought (the train
Now sliding slowly forward), *needs no action
On my part*, as he watched for the row
Of bungalow lights along the hill to acknowledge
The lake's reflection. Sure enough, they lined
The road for half a mile, waiting to illuminate
The path of a dignitary who has not yet arrived.
Not for a couple of thousand years, anyway.

IX

If God has a failing, it is surely His anger.
Or Hers? Knowing God, surely we'd know His/Her gender?
Would we be slower to presume we knew His/Her emotions,
And, more uncertain than ever, apply ourselves to devotions,
Seeking to know God's will, rather than His/Her mood?
Such knowledge, surely, would be neither bad nor good.

X

This won't do at all, this back-tracking,
The search for a source that could explain
The character's motive when he drew the *ingénue*
Into the picture he had painted for the old
Couple whose farm by the canal would make way
For a resort if they agreed a price.

The simpering
Teenage grandchild, who smoked reckless amounts
Of hashish with him in the hayloft, loved
The old dears she was staying with for the summer.
She liked incense too, the wee room under the roof
Like a chapel on a feastday, ribbons of blue-grey smoke
From five or six joss-sticks burning, one in each
Corner and two by the bed.
                              The grandfather came
Halfway up the narrow stairs and shouted *Fire! Fire!*
And the girl, so stoned she had no idea who
Was shouting, jumped out the dormer window
And fell twelve feet into the lavender.
                                    The protagonist
And puppeteer-impresario of this ugly farce,
Dealer in dope and incense, was watching
From the canal bridge as the ravelled cords
Of his puppets collapsed into the smoky scenario,
For want of a motive—he too merely a puppet,
A hero-villain from vaudeville, reliant on
His unreliable inventor to pull strings.

        XI
Use your imagination! Do I remind you of Anyone?
How will you wrest an answer from the void
Without considering the source of this information?
Sell everything of value, buy a plentiful store
Of corn for the others, who believe everything
Their delicate senses receive from every breath
They draw, though it be from the angry desert.

Come, these devious looks, what ease have you,
Burdened with anguish by these short-lived lies,
This vanity, this resentment? Your release begins,
However late, when you rise and leave
The counting-house, when the lash of Self drives

You into the field to lie down and willingly
Cover yourself with its green blanket.

XII

Cat plays with a beetle in the carpet,
Then insists on going out. Dark
Of the moon: the air solid darkness.
The beetle's shiny black carapace
Has entered the cat's metaphysic.
She is not one to analyse, though.
Thin and jumpy, instinct keeps her
In touch with the occult dance she joins
When sensible Dog is sniffing at mischief,
Barking at the merest lightening
Of dark's burdens, those yearnings
Among the rhododendron and cotoneaster
That send him into rhapsodies of sniffing.
But God at three in the morning
Wants peace, a break from the usual,
And quickly restores the stony dark
To block any further commerce between
Knowledge and kindness, the feral and the tame.

XIII

The distant delayed croon of the transatlantic jet
Reminds the exiled poet of the gale's hoarse roar
In the chimney the first night he dozed
Fitfully under rafters and slates in the cottage,
Half-ruined, half-buried in alder and furze
Halfway up a West Wicklow valley, bandit country
By all accounts, from time immemorial.

All of which is half-true, he realizes,
And, being a poet, does not stay to analyse
But rushes on with the fading jet-sound until
He can reach the confusion of sense—the seat,

Twenty-one C, the aisle, won't recline, nor would
The padded nylon sleeping-bag on chairs
In the stripped living-room offer rest,
So that the slightest resemblances magnify
His recalled anxieties; this montage,
Left here, half-finished.

XIV

And lest you, God, be afraid this is yet another
Resignation, with which you are only too familiar,
In lieu of service due, or stop-gap waiting
For further instructions, here it is in writing
On lined white copy-book paper and indelible
Black ink to make sure it is legible and durable,
A permanent document, like a peace treaty
Signed and sealed on a stone at the gates of the city,
First by the vanquished, pride written dismally off
In a few paragraphs agreeing to the loss
Of everything worth a damn, signifying the end
Of the idea there was an ideal to defend;
Then by you, victor, *In Hoc Signo*, the scrawl,
Large and careless, of one whose word is law.

XV

A sail off the Fastnet Rock leans
Into the wind, a white triangle
On the tilted sparkling green-blue
Merging of air and water.

An old map of the coast
From Hook Head to Brandon,
With the sea for three miles east-
South-east, displays a fierce
Dolphin cocking its tail
At the legend, *Here Be Monsters*.

Yes, and beware too the Ides
Of every season, even August,
When young Cantillon sat becalmed
In the lee of Fastnet for forty hours,
Saw monsters, went mad and swam
To the iron rungs below the lighthouse,
But had no strength to climb.

XVI

The terns have blown inshore
On the whim of a southeaster,
Force six, over the mountains.
On the lake's slate-grey screen
They devise elaborate white
Invasions, screeching wildly,
Then diving straight down,
Wings tucked, at the shallows.

Shadowy minnows scatter
Across the erratic mud-water,
But the terns are undeceived,
Circling, screeching, excited
Now that they understand,
And as quick as they arrived

They fly off along the shore
In twos and fours, fixated on
The wind's fickle will, that won't
Permit them to be still
For even a moment's reflection.

Envy

Not now, said Augustus to his favourite poet Horace,
Who was approaching the army general not long raised
To the new purple, the new throne, the borrowed
Divinity. So the poet bowed low and quickly left,
Satire in hand, to take horse and ride from Rome
Up to the Sabine hill he knew the Gracchi coveted
For a retreat of their own. Merely a hillside farm,
As Maecenas measures these things; but Horace felt
Cossetted.

      He vowed to stay out of the city
Until Reason gained a foothold on Olympus
And Jove, benign and suave, to whom even Caesar
Was obliged to pay respect, if not homage,
Attended to the lessons Psyche teaches
Even godly minds. That fair spirit took
A hand in Rome's fortunes, so the warrior-king
Could climb into the gilded chariot
After another victory against the Gauls.
(Libations, of course, to the gods for their role.)

      But neither Jove nor Reason spared the poet
From the Emperor's embarrassing attentions.
The city claimed his time, the farm neglected.
Caesar admired his wit, so Horace gave him
Satires aimed at others who could afford
To suffer lighthearted jibes disguised
As wise conundrums.

      Released at last, he gave
The *Carmina*, abundant harvest, all the time
They needed to bear fruitful tidings to
The troubadour, the courtier, the happy rationalist,
The solemn elegist, the envious sycophant
Writing these lines while he waits for Psyche to call.

from *Observations* (1960)

Baptism

In the quivering candleswell
The cross priest round frail cradlecries
Braces faith in chrismsmell
Where in sponsor's arms each lies.
Hope rumbles in his monotone:
Where falls the seed that he has sown?

The wrinkled deacon grimly knows
This tarnished ceremony glows
On twelve wry souls queued for the font
While he's candleposed in front:
But, telling love in each grey phrase,
His pose betrays his thoughtless gaze.

Fresh from elemental pains,
Shrill to live, they howl and grin:
Still blameless for their common sin,
Yet born to sin, each brow disdains
Christ's spittle to unfurl their eyes.
—Satan thunders in their cries.

November

Smoke
In the coruscating air
Drifts
Like a prayer I said yesterday,
Between heaven and
My ineffectual soul.

A Liberal Education

On my demesne here
Strays the fragment of a path
Through thyme and thistles gone to seed.

This enigma knew
A little order when
A gardener railed at the stony clay.

The Jesuits planted
Tulips for a comely Spring
And orchards for their Autumn fruit.

Now reigns again
The eglantine around,
And poppies bleed
Above the half-obliterated rows.

American Papers Please Copy

His days eroded like an old estate
Vultured by revolutionaries, until
They sent wreaths and flowers
And filled a cavalcade
Of sad smiles in limousines
Held up by traffic in Phibsboro.

They coughed their yesterdays
Into their handkerchiefs
Behind the chauffeur's inscrutable shoulder.
He knows by heart their soulless
Pandering to a soul they praised
Only out of policy: halfmeant,
Halfmeaning phrases that scan the lives
Of the dozen he's seen buried in a month.

from *A New Address* (1965)

A Sadness Coming Over Me
Homage to Samuel Beckett

Playing the wrong music for public places
Piping out of tune
Where tired dancers pass fretfully across stage
I among the woodwind
Dare not articulate for fear of letting truth
Corrupt their ragged innocence
Or worse if they discovered in my brilliant
Waistcoat pocket
Those gems I store
For the beneficiaries of my estate
My reason and my dreams
And flatten them
In the loose earth under their pompous feet
Where they will lie soon enough
God knows when my sweet breath
Blows for the last time to thrill
The leaves in my neighbourly trees
No I will not play
A shadow in their flattering cabbage gardens
I will define my terms
When I have acquired an olive grove
To encompass solitude

A New Address

Waves, grey and misty, made a dungeon
To shut in our walks last winter.
Snow on the foreshore
Glistened after Christmas.

I

My silence, too long self-imposed,
Stretched beyond vain acres
Into Spring, a time for voicing.
I was not heard, and I was to blame.

Impediments found themselves niches
In long corners of a framework
Like vacant spiderwebs, collecting dust.

Now, in St. Martin's Summer, comes
A last perchancing rush with the pen
Gallivanting at the disarray
And ill-humour of a house
Waiting to be put in order,
Not by these quick licks,
Shifty and skyranting as before,
Nor by insouciant sabreswiping
(Though much needed among the weeds
Clinging and cascading where they will
About these fabulous gardens),
But by care, learning, piety—gifts
Left out of all my wills.

II

Well, then. Breathe in. Who spares
The institutions primed on the droppings
Of the rich in charity poor in love
Parentally controlling all our feasts
Lest feast-days fast for their encouragement?

God help poor priests who flock
At evenings less devout than rhyme
Can reason them to devotions! My last year,
Confined as I was to a TB ward and full
Of sore disenchantment and enlightenment
Breeding twins in me, a bout of reason
Froze me in a womb of slow conception.

Leaving behind the pleasures of Blanchardstown,
I called upon a parish presbytery,
The house next door to God's, with polished brass,
A square of grass, and sprinklings of nasturtiums
Or What-have-you in behind forbidding railings.

A forbidding maid—a maiden maid, I'd swear—
Reluctantly inched open the confessor's door,
Enquired my obviously sinful purpose there,
Then, curt and disapproving, led me through
Her clinical cleanliness to a solemn room,
All polish and that sneaky atmosphere
Of well-to-do you're not supposed to mention.

In comes the man in black to save my soul—
And save his too: his holy orders are
To that effect. They graced him little, though,
For, through the Roman spit and celibate polish
And virtue's shirt so rigorously collared,
Ruddy cheeks and strong jawbone declared him
Native of limestone Tipperary acres,
Betraying by his sturdiness
The polish of his parish.

Was I absolved?
God alone knows.

III

Breathe out. Inhale again
The languid air. Near midnight.
Shadows curtain the garden's
Intimate flourishing.

A middle-aged woman, head jerking,
Limbs angled into a fretful stance,
Attracting attention in College Green,
Lit a song in me for a social leper....
And now it lies about me, shreds
Of vacuous compassion.

Scene Two: cheap cinema platitudes
From girls brought up in convents
Renowned for their refinement
Passed me, heeded. I passed, needing,
Not a scourge for clumsy nunneries,
But quires of foolscap for benign
Hymns to comely crossroad maidens.

IV

I lit a bonfire, piling
Refuse against a wall.
A million dying woodlice,
Worms, spiders, centipedes,
Earwigs, beetles, ants,
Crawled and kicked in the flames.

Outlandish, the poor: they harvest love
And sell it cheap as dirt from barrows,
Raucously proclaiming how they love
Nothing better than honest poverty.
My love I give freely, and cherish theirs.

There y'are love, shilling a punnet
The lovely strawberries. Lovely red apples!

My city's vistas captivate;
She is skilful with her places.
Her canal is known to poets and whores
(Separately trading);
Touring cameras chew Christ Church
Into two dimensions.

But little lanes with railings,
Window-boxes, *bric-à-brac*
Unrequited in a dealer's shop
And listening faces and behind
The Rathmines copper dome
Are litanies to comprehend
Empty glories all my own.

V

I attacked the thistle and dock,
Sharp glass refracting light.
When the weeds were felled, I laid
A green lawn over the clay.

My house is laughable really: doors
Open the wrong way; water-pipes
Rattle, every wall's uneven, restless.

Whitewash the wall and paint the wood:
Just so. I will renounce the home
That would deprive me of my books.

So I'll hang chintz curtains, order flowers,
And sturdy furniture.
With soap and wax I'll burnish
The bright day with my hope.

A rose dips from a neighbour's wall;
I gather his apples when they fall.
A noble armchair is my throne,
And here, at least, I'm on the phone.

VI

Catch-penny phrases litter my brain
Yet bring assuagement. When the din
And sway of tortuous days oppress,
Even the saintly would settle for less.

All the parades I saw,
And life's trite charades,
And the littered façades....
A lover's thighs below
A skirt in disarray....
One morning, too late
For love, I mourned
Among the tramps reclining
In their grandiose vocational
Postures in St. Stephen's Green.

Ring the herald bell
Cast out all precious devils
Swing incense alleluia
The scant night sees me home.

Canal at Easter

Bulrushes, disarmed by frost,
Now a defenceless summer aegis,
Lay bare the debris decaying
Along the lapping shallows.

Under water, refuse
Assumes a magic movement;
Plates, slates, caducent metal
Bejewelled for their new lives.

Pinched, hoared with dust,
The hawthorn's lazarine fingers
Forage listlessly among
The Maundy waters.

From black cadaverous gates
The splendid terror spurts
In thundering expiation
Of the city's discarded sins.

The primordial mallards
Are mating. Tentative,
They etch in the effluence
Their cyclic path.

The Rain His Prison Bars

Closing the gap,
Moving unhurried through drenched cattle
To a yard littered with rivulets,
A sackcloth over his stooped shoulders,
He brings with him to an odorous room
Odours of rain on the fields he loves.

Crouched hands at the open door
Of the iron stove, the steam
Wisping around him, he hears
Lowing, fowl's piping, rain against
The thatch and solid walls embracing him.

His prison is of his elements, his lights.
We scratch initials on papers to prove
We read them, and deem our square of sky
Enough when we hear the slamming of doors
Of other cells along the corridors.

Stella

Cassiopeia stirs
With fond escort.
He rolls in his head the drums of love
Under her influence;
A still figure in the garden,
Scarcely observed where he stands
In darkness among dissolving
Summer flowers.

The swan pierced by an arrow lies
Immortal on sharp stars
Above the bowed head ringing with the tones,
Vibrations, plangent chords of love.
About him, night sounds:
A leaf touching his shoulder
Whispered, descended, dying
At his feet.

Orion's hectic music
Plays *perpetua mobile*
For the dancing trees,
Sensuous black branches posing
In sibilant mime the thunder in his blood.
Breath crept from his lips
And fled into the sky
Carrying love's dispatches.

Taurus, urgent
In that sky's sculpture, commands
His gaze to rise and meet
The rowdy challenge of his beam.

Allowed a leniency, denied a right, he bends
Again his head and turns eyes down,
Reflecting the inclination of the spheres
That hold his secret.

At a far window, Stella rests
Fine brow against the pane
And mingles under Hesperus
Her breath with his.

Audience

They were all there for the good of their souls,
Arms folded, knees crossed in communion,
Teaching themselves to be beholden.

They were all there with their claws stretched,
Awaiting a prey to pounce on,
Iliad and Eliot tangled and thoughtless.

They were all dumb with a movement of whispers
In considerate pauses of poets;
They were all harmonious, empty and tiresome
As the plasterwork swathing the ceiling.

Sunday

In the avenue—toy bricks arrayed
On a nursery floor, the child's idea
Of how a street should look—
Stiff families move out
Through stiff metal gates,
Brisk to Mass, coppers for the plate
Held in tight pockets, Peter's pence.

Bracing mouths and eyes to meet
Too close neighbours, they plant out
Remote platitudes, shrugging
The armory of manners
Closer to their collars:

Half geared for conversation, half
For their consciences wrangling with
Immensities of the week's devotion.

from *The Revolution (1966)*

a verse satire in five parts,
performed by the Lantern Theatre Company,
Dublin, May 1966,
directed by Patrick Funge.

Prologue

NARRATOR (a man of mature years, a substantial "presence"):

Doomed—I suppose for sloth—I've crossed my path
With those broad highways of the righteous
Of all denominations, sects and creeds
As seldom as possible. Those demure divines,
Toting their tomes and dreary manuals
Of directions for the approach to paradise,
Can save their grace to lubricate their own
Engines of salvation. For my part
I keep to my bed, a most salutary haven
Wherein to study learned dissertations
On the Arts, Philosophy, Politics and such,
Pondering at my ease in the odorous blankets
The threads from which our mortal mantle's woven.

Betimes, for recreation, I bestir
Myself to venture down our Capital streets,
Sent by those texts upon an aimless quest.
By Tolka's polluted waters have I gone down,
And Dodder's rat-infested banks and groves;
By the Liffey, celebrated in song and story
For the stench of ordure rising like holy incense.
By Grand and Royal canals, those cesspools where
Poets before me have mournfully meditated,
Have I gone; and thence to bestride a barstool
And bend a weary elbow in Dougan's Bar.

One neon twilight, casual years ago,
Chance, the oldest whore in Christendom,
Draped in her patchwork evening gown, paid me
A visit while I breathed those boozy vapours
And introduced me, with a wicked smile,
Keeping her cracked lips sealed, to the craven four

Whose antics, at her prompting, would soon disrupt
The peaceful squalor of our metropolis.
In the smoky haze around the potbelly stove
That glowed between two lavatory doors,
Four youngish, clerkish types growled in a powwow,
Drinking pints of stout and giving out guff
About the louts who ran our state's affairs.

A lanky *Auditor,* senior by some years,
His forehead a half-inch broader than the others'
And given to more sombre clothes than theirs,
Impatiently presided, or himself harangued
The other three, who listened with surly expressions.

Beside him, like a redhaired teddybear,
Restive with lice and dandruff, a *Tote Cashier*
Leaned sideways, shrugging impatiently
While the others recounted their bitter histories.

Watching the Auditor, reading his lips, poised
With attentive beak, head cocked like a heron
Waiting to catch a minnow in murky waters,
Was the one who pored his dusty hours away
Apprenticed to a dry *Solicitor.*

Secretary for this group, *Librarian*
By occupation—so his smile betrayed,
Leaden with tedium, stiffened by deception—
A chinless, shoulder-stooping, shifty ghoul—
Nodded and pursed his lips at all being said
While gluttony overcame his longing for bed.

Each sucked on a pint of frothy black stout and waited
His turn to relate an example of the general rot
Spread by the current government. The Auditor
Was first to speak, concealing calmly in calumny
His closest purpose—no less than absolute power
Over the State—not for reform, not for personal profit,
But to wield power, this terrible abstract concept
That heated his blood, steadied and readied him
To chance anything and everything to attain his ends.

Listen in, if you will, as he begins to unfold
His devious scheme, his plan for a great upheaval,
As a corkscrew twists loose the cork from a potent bottle.

from *Draft Balance Sheet* (1970)

Making Repairs

Poetry Workshop, Arkansas, 1966-68
i.m. James Whitehead

Vulcan is up there, hammering
With chiselled fist on a manuscript
As if it would yet make a weapon
For a war of gods; but forgetting
The war is over, lost
To Mammon's unfeeling host.

Icarus is down here, trying
To fix his wings, sighing
As the wax melts in the heat
Of his own hand. He cannot repeat
That first ecstasy of flight,
Or his first failure's bleak delight.

The Passion

In 1964, a French film unit brought back from Kivu Province in the Congo a sequence shot in a village which had been recaptured from rebel forces. Among many instances of brutality during the "questioning" of the villagers, the film showed one young man, bound hand and foot, being kicked to death by the government soldiery.

Before the dutiful soldiers came up to Gethsemane
Christ wept and asked his father to forego the trial,
Then said, *Thy will, not mine.* There's little enmity
About these soldiers as they smile and smoke
And nonchalantly kick at the closed eyes: their style
Grows out of every soldier's duty while they poke
At the writhing loins till they are still, and while
Their sergeant waves at the camera, and while they spit
Carelessly into the dust around the matted hair.
                                        Christ spoke
Of love from his cross, but still I cannot fit
Golgotha's theme to the savage sermon evoked
By the sergeant shrugging, by the pistol shot to the head,
By the turning away of the soldiers, by the grit
From the street that dries the quiet blood.
                                        If Christ is dead,
Has he not yet risen? Or is this on the screen a skit,
A playful allegory from history's frivolous masque,
A killing as gratuitous as that in which Christ bled
To redeem this sin? Is it his Father I should ask
Why this should earn for soldiers their daily bread?
What is His mercy? Should I condone the soldiers' smiling too?
The villager's bound heels and wrists have something to do,
God, with the reasons I do not believe in You.

Map

In six-inch scale, the Mayo baronies
Cover half the wall above my couch.
Bog and mountain, tarn and cascade: I trace
These abrupt crazed contours where the gannet sweeps
Round rock and cliff, the bay below groaning, the wind
Cudgelling the coarse grass flat as it drives inland.

Here, on the narrow slope between crags and sea,
Clan fought clan, the misty cliffs over them,
Searock a false step below, and the Atlantic gale
Drumming their shields with shafts of rain. No peace
Ever visits that shore; no worth in that stony ground.

Papers everywhere—piled onto tables and shelves—
Accounts marked overdue, old magazines, failed poems.
A room occupied too long. Inertia. I should
Give up scanning the map, prone here on the couch,
And like my father take rootless flight.

He was an inconstant collector—Spode jugs,
The Complete Works of George Moore, trout flies—
Fads, pawned off in time to pay for new caprices.
In his last place, the apartment in Beirut,
A dozen Persian rugs lapped over each other,
Auctioned off when he died. I stole from his estate
The bronze gesturing Shiva with the little smile.
Is it tribal greed has driven us over the earth…?

Was it greed for possession of these salty crags
That drove them at each other, wave after wave,
Yelling, stumbling through bulrushes and mire
Between Achill and the Bellacorick bog?
No one knows the outcome; no one has named the victor.
Place of the Great Slaughter in Irish on the map.

When the blighted stalks
Lay cracked and brown above
The harrow-rows, the lean
Poets ceased their singing
By the blackened hearth and sought
The exile ship in the cove;
Or death released them from
Mourning the pestilence
That shadowed every face,
And rage against the tyrant
Whose greed fostered famine
Rattled in their throats.

Rage swept them across the Vistula, Danube, Elbe,
Before they had names for rivers. They hammered
Images into bronze and gold to shield them
For the crossing to the Isles of Bliss they dreamt
Beyond the storms. Now they have spanned oceans
And given their names to places they stayed in
Hardly long enough to light a fire or dig a grave.

My father learned to navigate the old way,
By the stars—could fly a course
From Ganges to Euphrates—knew half the globe
From the air. The Ides of March: taking off
From Tehran, his plane crashed at the edge
Of a place that is called in Persian *Desert of Salt*.

In this littered room I have toyed
With thoughts of flight to such exotic places
As those my father mentioned in his letters—
"Twelve thousand feet above the desert,
Getting close to Alexandria...." But instead
I buy books and sometimes read them; or doze
To Haydn when I try to write; or put down
The pen, lost for words, considering the map,
The warriors roaring, the *caoineadh* echoing.

> The gannet settles
> On the narrow ledge
> Between rowdy waves
> And rain-laden clouds.
> On the slope of great slaughter
> A mountain ash raises
> One stricken limb.

A Poem in Place of a Lecture
Or Vice-Versa

This morning, friends, the blackboard will be black
Behind my skull: your eyelids will be slack,
And I could wearily cajole from you, or you,
Slow answers to dull questions; or grow annoyed
Earnestly deploying on the black void
Lyra's measured stars. But I must learn anew
To cope with darkness: these voids won't do
As palps where I could plot the dusty lore,
The diagrams, the arty emblems you ignore,
Your blood too thin to tick into the brain
The winged horse mustered from the sod
To be the Muses' pet, a demi-god
High in black heaven. I will not strain—
The chalk crumpling, your eyelids flickering—to explain
Why ignorant men pricked darkness full of scars
And gave them godly names, and called them stars.
You quench whole constellations on the black
Walls of your skulls; arts you dishonour die.
The sky will go black and Hippocrene run dry
Before I will fix one light in your blind skulls this black
Morning, friends. The blackboard will stay black.

Draft Balance Sheet
Dublin-Galway, 1966

A shambling urban prospect
Spreads under gathering clouds.
Pale grass climbs through derelict beams,
Breaks from old basement flagstones,
Advances over scarred ground.

New movement of men and gear
Will throw up girder and glass.
In the hoarding's shadow, a slack wind
Plucks at discarded wrappings, crumpled foil,
Flicks over gleaming rubbish.

Clouds build like Atlantic rollers
Over the street's sad scape. I turn my back
On the view that hardly a month ago
Stretched a Palladian vista to the Dublin hills.
The heart won't ease. Nothing I scribble down

Accounts for leaving. Our tickets are bought
For the journey, a month's rent in advance—
Things will improve if we go—our wings to spread—
Yet the aching for home burns as if home
Had been across water these past twenty years.

The skyline climbs against the dropping sun;
Bridges arch dun water; the city's only
Skyscraper strikes up from the Liffey wall.
Old rooftops gather westward, black and sheer
Across the red-gold sky like sea-carved rocks.

Streetlights flare along the quays and tumble
Like yellow flags churning in murky water
Past barracks, breweries, brothels, old domes,
Past the Ballast Office, the Custom House, and out
Past Bailey's winking light to the dark sea.

The train grinds round the loopline over the bridge.
We rumble through drizzle. The cemetery wall,
The drenched bog. We pick up speed between stations
As misgivings mount in the heart. Then grey
Galway stone. Then the rocking launch to the liner.

The western panorama: village lights
Pinned like moths on the low receding coast.
Connemara frets the sky that still glows
Faintly, even near midnight. Then all is sea.
Drunk exiles sing, and the great ship rises
Near Aranmore, lit up like a Disney palace.

The stewards are blond Norwegians; passengers
From Denmark, Berlin, or returning to New York.
We're under way, and the heave of ocean in a gale
Drives me sick to the cabin. These days, these years,
And the island behind us still exacts
Her tribute: this rage, this love.

These Fine Mornings

These fine mornings, your voice
Mingles with sounds, near and far:
The traffic's din through all highways,
The sparrows under the eaves,
The cricket's antic drubbing.
Your voice says, "Be gentle."

I close my eyes. Your lips move
On mine. I move in your breath
As the light limbs of saplings renewed
In spring breezes. Your voice mingles
With the wakening clamour on highways,
The chorus that swells in my veins.
Your lips move. I'm gentle.

Arresting Officers

Out on the street, in gusty rain,
A ragged vagrant, drunk or insane,
Sheltered under a lintel. Disgrace
Had darkened his features, lined his face.
Pitiably mouthing, changing stance,
Raking the street with his fierce glance,
He shivered in the doorway, until
The Law, with slightly ridiculous skill,
Surprised and dislodged him. With an oath,
He lurched off, the guard behind, and both—
Grim cape and wild jacket—turned to the right
Round the corner and out of sight.

I reach for a pencil and clean page,
Ordering lines that might engage
Tramp and guard in fable or vision;
Make art of the action's drenched precision:
The stout-shouldered guard in his slick cape
Moving the tramp like a puppet takes shape
In rugged metrics, neat word-play.
But as I write, to my dismay,
The burly motion, the surly grimace—
The incident's import—disintegrates.
Rain rinses the empty street. I find
Scene and characters slipping out of mind.

FAYETTEVILLE, ARKANSAS, 1967

The fat butt of the pistol
Sat level with his kidney,
Arranged so it could nestle
In the gut above the hipbone,
The wood polished with handling,
Snug in black leather, like a pet.

His jowl worked gum, eyes kindling
As a boy, shirt open, head
Rolling, loose underlip wet,
Knees buckling, shackled wrists
Like vines, hands scarred, was led
Past him into jail. His fist
Jerked on the desk; he shook his head

Slowly. "Called me sonofabitch," angling
His forearm from the desk. "I hit
Him so hard it still hurts, right there"—
Rubbing his trigger finger on fat
Knuckles. The rookie dispatcher stared.
The other straightened, hand fondling
The gun. "Ain't been one like that yet,
You hurt 'em a little, they get scared."

from *After The Blizzard* (1975)

Examination

You make me dizzy with lust.
Watching as you write,
Ballpoint alive in your fist,
The line immaculate
From breast to palpable breast,
I'm taking nervous note
Of how much you'd invest
(Don't stop to meditate)
Of thrust and counterthrust
If we would share a sheet.

Your fingers tire, resist
The throbbing pen. You're stiff.
You stretch. This easy test
On *Medea* brings you grief.
With all your treasures blessed,
You still will make an F.

Vivaldi in Venice
(La Cetra, Op. 9, No.6)

I

Arched corridors. Bare white walls.
Sunlight, slanting off water, caught
On the dead Redeemer's hand
In a niche by the chapel door.
The marble hand, long, slim,
Glossy from pious stroking.

The girls in grey uniforms, bows
Poised over their polished viols,
In the great vaulted room
Where waterlight dapples the ceiling.
Under their lowered eyelids, sins
Unnumbered. The whitehaired *maestro*,
Hands raised as for a blessing,
Smiles, "Begin."

II

Violas are moaning, a harpsichord chiming
Chords he made simply to please.
And the Emperor nods like Apollo,
Lulled by the resonant cellos.
Divine violin,
Sing low, sing in—
To orphan, to emperor, bring heartsease,
In court and convent redeeming,
Redeeming sin.

III

Under the humming *continuo*,
Needle on spinning disc,
The globe with its face to the sun,
The sun-god's golden lyre,
And orphan Ophelia singing.
Nodding, humming, the last
Habsburg surveys the salon,
The rustle of charmed ambassadors.

The needle sticks on a high note,
A strange bleating repeated.
The smiling, clouded, stops.
Sin, Madness, Grief
Enter, screeching and screeching.

The Exile's Recurring Nightmare

PROLOGUE

Not for me the Crusader cross:
I carry the common badge
Of exile, an uneven wedge
Of geese wild on a field of loss,
Legend, MEA CULPA, on its edge.

Desert, strewn with rock.
In the tawny dust, my own track.
The sun's unblinking eye.
Then ahead, white wings sweep
Up: lifting, lifted. *Go back,*
Go back, I heard their wild cry,
Nor woke from that troubled sleep.

MEMOIRS OF A SON OF ERIN

The Island:
My Lady of the Rocks,
The yachtsman's laughing daughter!

Behind the harbour, where sharp rocks
Gnashed their teeth at low cloud
Rushing to sea on a fair breeze,
She found the one smooth place
And sat enthroned. On the shore,
No more than the cast of a crab-line away,
I kept my place below her,
Spying, as she laughed,
Throwing her head back, laughing,

Her shadowy cleft. Cruel God!
Threaded by that thin green line
Angled down to the grey sea's floor,
I feared God would send a great Crab
To fasten on my baited hook
And drag me to damnation
For longing that my Lady
Of the Rocks would laugh, parting her thighs
Under her holiday skirt—
I would sail on her father's ketch
Past Rockabill and Lambay
To the ends of the earth, lusting
After my Lady of the Rocks!

The Nation:
The noble Plunketts of Saint Anne's:
Howth's lilac, forsythia, the sea-breeze;
Sleek horses cantering in their pastures;
Set for an idyll by Watteau, the belvedere.

His Lordship a champion of cooperatives;
His mansion, a Palladian jewel, commandeered,
Gutted by a drunken quartermaster
To conceal his paltry embezzlements.

The hawser twangs taut, the tractor backs
Over the weedy terrace. The great gable groans,
Bricks spill down, a blackened plaster cherub,
Wings open above the rubble, plunges.

The Church:
Bishop Patrick slew a goat in this holy village.
Born under that horned sign; in the saint's church baptised.

The sacristan swung us high on the knotted bell-rope

When he rang the Angelus out over town and tide.
We brought the old cripple food vouchers, a blanket.
Her cabin stank of excrement, gangrene. She cursed us.

Our Holy Mother the Church is the haughty nun
Whose-steel-rimmed spectacles flash, whose pearl
Rosary beads clink in the black folds of her crotch.

JOURNEY WITH A CONJURER
(i.m. Eustace Malcolm)

That prodigal road! By rampant hawthorns you braked
The noisy old Adler, and we walked out on the bridge
Below the salmon-weir. The glistening arcs
Of blue-black salmon over foam, their bellies flashing,
Smacking the brown waters, called Leixlip
By the horned Norse. As we left,
Two frowning swans took command.

In Kinnegad, a barmaid gone on magic,
Maid of a thousand calf-eyed smiles. You told her
A wedding-night joke, palmed a coin and plucked it
From behind her jewelled ear; she whimpered
With delight. In the morning she brought goatsmilk
And two speckled eggs she'd stolen herself from the nest.

White spume, black rocks in the cove-mouth: Donegal
In a roaring gale, low cottages hunched in the wind.
Two days in the empty hotel, the Atlantic booming.
Guinness and brandy at eventide, talking
Of women, desire eddying with our cigar smoke
In the gloomy lounge, transforming the shy waitress,
Thin and plain, to a priestess of venery.

On the third day arose
To clearing weather, and Errigal's hoary cone
Stolid as lust ahead of us over the bog.

The Whiskey Priest Recites His Holy Office

Matins:
Beast-head in the mirror,
Goat with blunted horns.
Thread of blood in my spittle.

Song of blame, song of loss
Hums like beating wings
Inside that scowling skull
But will not pass these lips.

Hic est enim sherry for breakfast.
This shaking is my body.
They have stretched cords
To snare my feet.

Tenebrae:
Darkness heaves and spins.
I am at some edge.
A wild wing sweeps up—
My own breath. *Ho!*

This dark is memory.
My arms outstretched in the void,
I will my flesh to remember.

Sweat crawls on my thigh.
What sound takes shape in this throat?
Oh, low the word I'd sing,
Were I to sing.

Vespers:

In that desert dream I stared
A long time at the place
Burned black by those white wings.
Beside the bed, the empty
Wineglass, overturned.
A stain like blood on the floor.

The same dream, the same dream.
But tonight, where that cluster of rocks,
That cairn marking nothing, casting

No shadow, dissolved as I kept
Watch, and my track turned
Back through the yellow dust.

And out of great fear I awoke.

After the Blizzard

I

The air of an old song's in my head.
Wind puffs at the snow, sifting it
Into fences, tree-trunks, walls.
Straight above, a pale star winks out
In a clear streak of brightening sky.

Clouds pace over the house,
Making east with their burden.
Far down the hemisphere, light
Spreads between the clouds
As a door would open slowly
On a room left long disused.

What brought me here through the house?
You and the children sleep
Where still the dark is right.
Old tune, words faded, keeps
Pushing breath to my lips.

II

Behind the brightening cloud
The sun begins to climb
The low winter path
That will take it scarcely above
That crowd of swaying pines.

I cannot remember the name
Of the star above my house.
You and our sleeping sons
Are for a moment nameless, gone.
My song dies, the notes melting.
My breath is mist in cold air.

The garden lies deep under snow.
Shadows return from the dead
As the light grows. A bare branch
Angles up, a black arm
Raised against the gold cloud.

III

Not a sound. The house could be
A dark ship locked in snow
And I her captain, my breath
Spangled in strange light.

Where is the hawk and his victim?
Where is the mole and the cat
Who would devour him? The snow
Swept down through the dark

With the same power that made
The star grow pale and leave
The sky—quiet as the breath
Of my nameless song on the glass.

A bird among the pines
Pipes her single note.
The house is dark and quiet.
I recall two lines of that song:

Where'er you tread
The blushing flowers shall rise.
A song for summer. Time
To switch on lights, turn back

Through the house, ease open
The children's door; their breath
Like wind in snow. Sunlight
Grows pale gold in their window.

How Many Wings Has A Hummingbird?

for Judy Grossman

Egrets will slowly lift,
Fly white in the green like vowels
While we watch them rise,
Telling each other our white
Predictions. You moaned,
Not in complaint or desire,
But for pleasure in the scene—

The white oleander on the lawn's brink
Will hide the hummingbird
That your hand held,
Trembling, untamed,
That shock of red and green
Flying healed from your hand,
So swift your eye made magic
Of bird, flower, and lawn,
As I here make a wonder,
A world of honey and white,
For you, if you like, to inhabit.

Transfiguration and Death

I

He broke off all utterance.
Refusal and consent
Spun no more from his mouth,
Webbing the citizens.
Passing the last time among them,
He frowned at their salutes.

They watched him reach the bridge;
Then, like spittle in sand,
They turned back into the town.

II

The road sighed into the forest.
Fir-fronds combed his hair.
The bridge went down behind him.
Grey mist collapsed the mountains,
His breath consumed in cloud.

The rivulet at his side
Carolled mysterious signals.
The water worked his footsteps
Loose from the sandy trail.

The boughs dissolved in fog.
Higher, the wind on bare rock
Howled; or he cried out to the wind.

III

Nothing but stone and mist.
He walked out on the rock.
In the blinding gale he heard
Water creeping through roots,
Whispering like a lover.

Fir-fronds webbed his hair.
He saw the road in the forest,
His raw footstep in sand.
Drowning, he saw the bridge.

Dust Devils

Drought. Grey spirals into hard blue
Seventy feet or more over Hartmann's field,
The dust he plowed last week, sticking to schedule
Even when the seasons don't. Come Sunday,
It'll be ninety days and nights without a cloud,
Never mind rain. In June a front went over,
Not a drop, but lightning fired the forest
West of town. Pillars of smoke in tall rows,
Rocks cracking wide in the heat, and the smoke
Thick as wool for three full days. Preacher said
The sweet dry stench of burn that kept the town
Making sour faces and coughing was surely of hell.

Yesterday, on the old county road, no more than ten
Feet ahead of the pickup, we watched one start
From nothing, rattling cans some kids threw there.
It swept across the old Metlock place, spun out
In the black-locust grove round the ruined house.
Harmless. You could stand in one, it would tease your hair.
Bad sign though, dry earth, dry air dancing together.
On the reservation over the river, they're counted
The spirits of dead braves, still waiting for peace.

Nothing to be done with our scrub land
But ride fence in the pickup, bouncing hard ground,
Trailing our plume of dust. In dry waterholes,
Our steps make small puffs, though we move slow.
Found a dead calf in the creek bed. Brown hide,
Pale bones showing through, meat and insides gone.
Dust powdered over the carcass by coyotes.
Every night, they howl closer to the house.
Old Stan, our wino hand, shivers at the sound.
I dream nights of those burning trees, the shouts
Of the firefighters; wake with a dry throat. Metlock

Quit his farm, they say, because he dreamt the house
He built of pine logs he cut himself was crushed
Under black boulders that grew from the seed he spread.
He dreamt of this, night after night, then drove off
From that solid house. It took ten years for the roof
To collapse, in the blizzards of 'sixty-seven.
They say Hartmann will be the next to fail, the stubborn
German, scattering seed and fertiliser on dust.
I'll stick it out, though the preacher scolds every Sunday
Of our sins turning the fields into the devil's playground.

Michael Collins

1903

On their lips are legends
Telling of heroes straddling
Glens and lakes of the island.
Halls ring with votive song.

The haughty woman has ceased to mourn,
And the maiden turns back from the shore.
The songsters have broken their silence,
And the youth goes abroad in his field.

1916

A man among his people,
Each face a tragedy, dark
Mouths in the gunfire,
Praying, praying.

A last defiant echoing shot
Hits home, and it is ended.
The shattered barricades yield
Their maimed idealists.

1922

Whose fanatic bullet sped
To split Michael Collins' head?
Usurers, bloated with bounty, breed
Dynasties, now he is dead.

1937

"Up Dev!" The gaunt electioneer
Stands ruthless on the lorry above
Faces turned blindly into rain.
His plunderers wait for their chances.

This alien mystic's on his knees:
Black serge and church candles
Attend the new men. Diligent
Hounds of commerce attend them.

1966

But whose fanatic bullet sped
To silence Michael Collins' voice?
Usurers bloated with bounty breed
In the silence after Collins' voice.

Witness

> *"Sometimes the witness is more strangely*
> *involved than the actor."*
> —George Garrett, *King of the Mountain*

I

What did she see on the train?
Two figures, blurred by speed.
Light from a flashing sign,
Or the flash of a driven blade?
Was there a victim mouth

Hollowed out by pain,
The other figure crouched,
Ready to strike again?

II

She felt, as she left the station,
Those shadows move in her head
From confusion to conviction:
The victim pale, half-dead,
As the flushed assailant hurried
To join the platform crowd....
She'd often seen these lurid
Murder scenes: the screen showed
The shadowy act carried out
In ways that left no doubt....

Two men, laughing and squabbling
Shouldered through the rumbling
Station behind her. She knew
They were killers, they must be! She grew
Wild-eyed, a Cassandra, babbling
Over and over, "I saw! I saw!"

III

Had I been on that train,
Then watched the weak in their vain
Struggle with the strong,
I wouldn't have been long
Staring at the whole
Masquerade before the pale
Complexions of the damned,
Murderous gestures framed
In fiercest colours, would reel
Through the brain a tale
So ancient and cruel—such a lie
As to transfigure every passerby!

For the Humanism Class at Fairchild Airforce Base, in Place of a Lecture on the Book of Job

"O remember that my life is wind: mine eyes shall no
more see good"—Job 7:7

Sunset. Look away to the airbase, far
At the western edge of the parched plain.
Stolid Stonehenge could tell time no better:
Sheer black slabs stand up to the red
Wall of the sky. Speed up. Close in.

From Rambo Road they grow to great
Black bomber fins, alert on the ramp,
Alert in their circle, awaiting the last
Word. Slow down. Look away. Look east
To the fallow field, to the moorhen squatting
On her nest in the reeds by the pond's edge.

Pick up speed again. Look ahead. Switch
On lights. Check the instruments, the green
Dials glowing, my hand easy
On the controls. Easy, easy to rise
High into whispering ether, to bank and roll
Over the darkening globe, to leave below
The black moorhen, the nest, the black
Circle of fins; to set course
Straight for the sun's red target.

Down in the headlights
A grey blur, a slight
Creature. A squirrel. Brake.
Too late. Stop. Look back.

All gravity brings me too late
To the body flattened, the head
Moving. Alive. It looks straight
At me in the tail-light's red
Glare. Take a stick
From the ditch and strike
Till the small black eyes glaze dead.

Look away, look away. All quiet
On the ramp where the bombers wait.
The car hums under its hood.
In gear. Pick up speed. Look ahead.

Rondel

After argument, the words slow down.
You, the accused, are revealed as innocent,
And I, the judge, must toss aside my gown,
                    After argument.

But I'd like to know exactly what you meant
By that last term of endearment—I must be *shown.*
Move to appeal! Your words misrepresent

The case, whatever you say—and it's well known
The naked truth will make this judge relent…
Or at least reduce the sentence to a frown,
                    After argument.

The Path

"...and when I speak, the images of all I speak of are present, out of the same treasury of memory; nor would I speak of any thereof, were the images wanting"—St. Augustine

It was our one flirtation with the winter:
Fiery eyes in a bush
Fleshed by our lights.
The dark way home brought us to that white edge.

The beast who watches lovers and curses them:
An old rage, a blunt pulse
In the brain, drove us
To rail against dark and cold. Its track roved everywhere.

A black form on the long ridge of Wright's Hill,
Haunched like an idol
Against the low clouds,
Stayed still as hunter or hunted when we passed,
Steering between high banks
Of drifted snow. One night
It attacked, leaping at our lights, eyes
Burning as it fell away,
Rolling, scrabbling on the ice.
Then the limitless white silence returned to path and hill.

The old ones told
Us what to do.
"Kill it, track it to its lair, its young, kill them too."
We remembered its eyes.
One of us, very old, blind, neither
Woman nor man, said nothing, hands
Stretched to the flames.
A widow fed small twigs, one by one, to the fire.
Heavy snow that night.

Going home, we saw
Its fresh trail beside the treacherous path.

The long line of men and youths abreast,
Black cyphers in the snow,
Hallooed, whistled, yapped
Like pups. None would give it an assured name,
Nor believe in more than one.
Our voices rang in cold air.
The spoor gave out on the windblown ice of the lake.

The women began to feel,
In the blood of lovers and sons,
The beast of the blazing eyes, hunter and hunted.
Old paths from house to house
Grew faint beneath new snow.
No one claimed to have seen it; only the tracks.
The blind one growled from the hearth:
"It will be there forever. You cannot live without it."

That was our one flirtation with the winter.
After the thaw, our cars,
Lights chewing tracks through the dark,
Sped the highways between our cities.
We named the animals,
Set names for everything,
Even for what made our hearts race
When we passed through the dark
Beyond our lights.

Famous Last Words

I

Who can I say dictated
How I should behave?
Socrates in prison, exhorting his friends
To the calm end, his death itself a criticism?
Or the nameless balladeer
Singing him 'Sergeant', a true familiar,
One to toss ale with? What matter?

I will sit here on the terrace,
Shaded by the kind vines,
Bowered on this marble bench,
From where the eye can stray without anxiety
Over the orderly park to the poplars there.
And when the fireball rolls to overtake me,
My shadow will be printed on the marble,
As perfect, as lasting, as any Pompeii mosaic.

II

Many have been misled
By enemy propaganda.
But I have studied all
The official pamphlets, followed
Their instructions to the letter,
Constructed a sturdy shelter
Deep under my home ground,
Stocked it well with canned
Rations, candles, books—
All the necessities
To survive, *survive*.

III

No doubt at the time of the disaster
I'll be in the usual condition, plastered,
Rutting on a whore, or listening to her chat.
Then a flash at the window, and that'll be that.

IV

That morning, my mother will call
From our doorstep, and I will leave
My friends where they climb and shout.

My father with huge legs and hands
Will come home and sweep me up.
He will hold me against his shirt,
And I will hear his heart.

V

But Clement, my boyfriend, the Executive,
You know? At Whatsitsname Incorporated?
He said that a settlement, a truce—
Something that meant peace, at any rate—
Was arranged today in Paris? Our President
Is talking to their Top Man? You'll see, the news
Tonight will show it all. He said the market
Was steady, there was no sign of panic?

VI

Spittle bubbling on tooth and lip,
Pulse in the strident throat—
Then that last harsh syllable when the names
Of the dead collapse in the memory.

Is that cry a question?
Knuckle and tendon organise
Into a fist to answer
The exhausted air.

If tongue and palate cried out,
What Lazarus would hear?
I am a mute sinew
Clenched against the sour air.

VII
A nursemaid, startled by a thunderclap,
Dropped me. I suffered, will suffer, nothing.

From this chair, this window, I have watched
The politico with his rabble, the surly mob marching,
The fashion models clinging to their fancy men—all
The vanities a city street can offer. And miracles too:

A blind man singing to the gathered throng,
And all forgot his blindness, for he sang
As if he saw a well-beloved face.

So, in that instant when the wall
Between me and the street blows down,
I will be smiling. I will be trying to sing.

from *Recital* (1982)

Ritual
for Paula

Before I offer the wood,
I whet my knife on a stone
With simple strokes, back and forth,
So. I disown these hands,
Empowered by laws that hold
Moon and tide to their pledge.
Steel and stone, flesh and bone,
The blade's light song repeats.
I test its edge on the stony
Heel of my hand before
I offer the wood to the knife.

I learn again to take pains
With simple things: to take
The knife in my better hand, so;
And the driftwood, already worn
By the steely waves to a shape
I recognise as if dreamt
While I rocked in those waves myself—
The wood in this hand, so.

The mask of one I recognise
Stares up from the wood. I begin.

Letter to Richard Hugo from Drumcliff

"You don't know what it's like to come after that man!"
—Brahms, *in re* Beethoven

Dear Dick, This kind of travel is cheap enough:
Hard a' starboard after a vexing nightmare,
And there I leave you—Mister Yeats at Coole,
Being severe with young poets on Lady Gregory's lawn;
Looking over his specs at a few bedraggled sheep
On the shore of the murky lake. And he counting them swans.

It's just a Byzantine canter through Roscommon,
A fearful county for tinkers, to Drumcliff.
A Philip Larkin chapel, half-buried in old trees:
Bland, tame Gothic of the Established Faith
That none of the neighbours give a damn about,
Keeping to their long-lipped superstitions,
Their guttural gossip making a natural prey
Of the ancestral rector—"He's a nice man, *but....*"
Half-starved mongrels worrying a lame sheep.

The embattled cleric: patrolling his neat grounds,
Pondering his fingernails, the only
Clean set in the parish; preparing to preach mildly
On "Prudence" again to his congregation of five—
Six, if you counted the deaf-mute poorhouse orphan,
His only convert, who was let ring the bell betimes
And weed the gentry's graves in the cemetery.

The peasantry? He sang them plain and cruel,
Dour and quaint; went sour on them, invented
A freckled ghost in tweed with a fly-rod and an ear
Cold enough to hear him out. He caught
Neither salmon nor trout himself; hated low bars;
His women all had double-barrelled names.
How could *we* move in *his* circles? His goddam gyres!

Randy laughter, hell! His lightest rhyme
Was strictly Big House—a bronze gong embossed
With gyres, moon phases, rose, rood, and tower.
Struck well, that great gong calls the lords and ladies
To their places at stage centre, *right.* He warped
The local colours of old saga, older *rann,*
To his own passionate, visionary weft,
As Virgil had for Rome in *her* decline.
Here, beneath white gravel, his immortal bone-white grin.

There's an old cross at the top of the graveyard lane.
The disproportionate head of the crucified figure
Wears the same dissembling agony-smile.
Some nameless monk, ten centuries ago,
Chipped the lichen off a great rock and cut
Him down to size.
So, that gorgeous gong resounds through Idaho....
Here, the tourist looks up from the arrogant plain stone
To a rook flapping in a galebent oak. It's like
Getting pissed off at Xerxes, as you say.

                                        Peace.
                                        Jim.

Cheiron

I

When I was a Curragh stableboy,
The filly Amaryllis sank
Her teeth in my shoulder as I bent
To ease her saddlegirth. This killed
In me the romance of these animals.

None of us without our marks from falls
Or rival whips—all of us deathsheads,
Lean as Hindu priests, awkward
As puppets when we walked the ground.
Many who learned nothing from their scars.

No horse I rode could fall. We took
Each fence for a prophecy to be
Fulfilled, into whose heart we galloped
Through the hallooing and cursing,
The boom of hooves, the inferno
Of gasp and snort, the bright flash of silk.

Then the breathless rocking
Over the cruel ditch, my fists
On the curving neck; then the tremor
Of landing, its head flung back
On the jolted shoulder, and my head
There, steadying. Then the surge
Under my knees for the next impossible hurdle.

II

The young broke ribs and thighs, clinging
To the old romance, great horse and gallant rider.
I offered them what I knew, but they could not accept.
Older, the intense tragedians of too many seasons,
They turned their unquenchable rage on their mounts
And drove them frothing into fences so beast
And man lay coupled in agony on the turf.

Once, at Phoenix Park, I heard
Unearthly sobbing, then the scream
Of the broken-back horse
Before the shot dispatched her.

With all affection dead, I learned their power.
I raced with the hope of winning, not to win.

III

To learn those powers I surrendered
My claim to manhood. At the starting gate
I bent my head to that place
Behind the ear, where the snout
Of the merciful gun would press.

Listening for the starter's call, eyes closed,
Murmuring to calm my horse, I saw, clear
And familiar as a dream, the course
And, winning or losing, the way we would cover it,

And at the edge of that vision
The others with their fearful chatter,
The blur of their colours—crimson,
Vermilion, cobalt, gold.

IV

I became a single sinew
Cleft to the galloping animal.

Once, three fences from home,
I pulled up just in time
On a gelding of Amaryllis'
Bloodline. But winning or losing,
No horse I rode could fall.

The Confession

To the grey rock below the silent park, in grey light,
The tide in its patient blind labour at last has yielded
The girl's form, waxen-white and rigid now.

She could no longer drive her lover to this murder,
Nor excite the youth who, finding her stretched there, is cold
With an unearthly fear, having discovered,

Once and for all, the mysteries of the flesh. He has covered
Her with his coat, so she lies like a Shrovetide effigy
Cast into the sea at midnight when lovers turn

Penitent. In the condominium nearby,
Shadows are wavering behind their venetian blinds.
Roused early from their beds by the forlorn sirens,

A few emerge on their verandahs, in bathrobes,
Hugging themselves, one watching through opera-glasses
While a doctor kneels to examine her, shaking his head;

And the sky stealthily brightens. The detective
Stares at the sea, waiting for his turn to look
For evidence. Figures vanish from their verandahs.

Her lover regards his hands as though another's
Clenched and unclenched before him, remembering
The low sound in her throat when her body opened

For love. He will never make the detective understand
How, cherishing her every breath, he surrendered
All that torment and desire to the quiet waves.

Persistence
for Robin Skelton, at fifty. RIP 1997

Sloth lounges at our table, the fat shade
Of Falstaff, wickedly entertaining bounder,
Always so candid, logical. Friendships founder
In the rough seas of our despicable trade—
Our homes in disarray, our hopes delayed,
Yet the Bitch Muse duns us for a more resounding
Line, no sooner delivered than she's hounding
Us for its match, and the account's never paid.

We know how the story ends, but a cold delight
Keeps us aloof from our own part in the play
While we balance (for a figure!) the soul's weight
Against the fleshed word, no better than spittle and clay,
In the Scales of Contradiction. Then we're the butt
Of Death's old joke again, and the devil to pay.

To his Host, Who has Asked Him to Stay Longer

We've learned in hard ways when we have to go.
There's nothing to explain, no one to blame,
And so much still to learn, we joke in sorrow.
Our children leave the house before their time,
Without a quarrel, casual, taking with them
Nothing to prize, and we may never know
What names they'll give their children. Nothing to do
But keep the house as neat as a chapel nave,
Fondle our friends' wives, let the wine flow,
Dance to old records, crooning of life and love.

We're sprightly enough, God knows, till the first ones leave.
It's a new kind of politeness we've let grow,
Going home while the party's in full swing to save
Our oldest friends the shame of letting it show,
This waking weariness that lays us all so low.
Tortured in our own beds by a hopeless fury,
We harp on how in youth we were always merry,
But can't remember now what made us so.

An Irish Bull (and a Botched Sestina)
for Jim Whitehead, Aet. XL. RIP 2003

Political passion is the poorest coin
We trade with. Slumped at the screen like resigned
Brokers or navigators, we're the last,
We pretend, to lend any value to words
So debased in the common exchange we feel them break
From their moorings in meaning when we bring them to meet

In metaphor—as if we could still make ends meet
Or tame any beast by such means. Words are coins
Thrown on a table to settle a debt, a sign
That nothing's settled. In the news at last,
Franco is dead. The smart men give us the word:
"He was good for Spain." Then a commercial break.

Old Farrell, my countryman, twenty at the outbreak
Of that war when we both were born, went south to meet
A fascist slug that sent him home lame. No coin,
Spanish or Irish, could straighten his step, resigned
As he was in his hatred, his only hope to outlast
Those fanatical, bickering, stomachy men, whose word

Is good for Business, always a good word
With upstarts and fascists. We've worked hard to break
Their code, to invest in a language that's meet;
But meanwhile the enemy we know has coined
A new name for himself and left no sign
That's the least inimical—no word that lasts.

Rage in Belfast, Beirut, L.A. The last
News item, Dow Jones bullish, then a word
From our sponsor. The doldrums, without a break
In sight. In the boredom of bad news we meet

Our worst enemy. Better to toss a coin,
Tails for the fascists, sure to come up, and resign

Ourselves like Farrell to a bitterness designed
For our own good to bankrupt the spirit. The last
Word for them from the newsman leaves no word
Unturned: *conservative*. Euphemisms break
Into spume to show us where the breakers meet
The rocks we've come too close to. But if the coin

Turns up the imperious head of coins, could we assign
Politics a lasting language, find the exact words?
Or, when the Beast breaks loose, turn back to meet it?

Timepiece

Needle and groove replay
A song I learned before
All songs became the same.
Something rotten at the core
Is winding its way in.

Stripping, I leave my clothes
And watch, as if they bore
A grudge against my skin.
Something to rot the core
Is ticking its way in.

It's not easy to wake up.
I'm bent double, with the floor
Shaking between my feet.
Something rotten at the core
Is eating its way out.

The headlines don't amaze.
Who's in power? We're not sure.
Soon we'll be in no doubt:
Something rotten at the core
Is eating its way out.

My friends have sent a card
With its false view of the shore,
The sea, the sky. They write:
*Something rotten at the core
Is eating its way out.*

Deposition of Harold Moore, Gardener,

AT THE INQUEST OF THE HON. MISS GLORIA
MADELINE HASTINGS, DECD. 21ST APRIL, MCMXXXVI

The topiaries were just my pastime.
It amused me to clip those evergreens
Into the shapes of begging dogs
Or crowing cocks, during slack times.
She praised me for those fancies,
Some said follies, but she hardly noticed
The trellis of climbing hybrid roses
Outside her study window,
That gave me so much trouble
Before the right yellow, dark
As gold, took the graft. I named
That one plant for her: Madeline.

Her whim was the croquet lawn:
Tiresome work, on my knees
Over every inch, weeding out
Dandelion, clover, scutch-grass;
Then the roller every day
For weeks, to get it as flat
As a table. I kept it that way
For years, though used but once.

At first there was plenty to do,
Limes along the drive to rescue
From a fungus, the walks to rake,
The banks of perennials
To thin out and make neat.
And when there was time, I tried
New hybrids in the hothouse,
Or clipped those green creatures.

She gave me a free hand,
Never a word of the cost,
Nor of praise either,when she strolled
Through the grounds in fine weather,
Stooping over her cane.
When she saw the Cupid
And the peacock and unicorn
I cut from the hedge between
The hothouse and the old stable,
She had to ask me my name
Before she could remark on them.

She sold the parkland for taxes
When the new government took over,
And paid off the indoor staff,
But kept me on. A few days' work
Was enough by then to take care
Of what remained—lawn and gardens
Between the house and the new road—
For half a season; though she seldom
Walked those paths any more.
I learned a new trade by taking
The bricks from the ruined stables
To wall out the sold land. On her side,
I planted a thick thorn hedge
And let it grow wild.

Next, she had to sell the gate-lodge
I lived in from the day she hired me.
I moved to a room behind the kitchen.
She taught me to cook plain meals.
We never ate together. Evenings, she
Made me read to her. I stumbled
Often over the strange words.

The house now stood among others,
Elm and beech cut down,
Replaced by bungalows,
On the land she had given up.
From behind the wild hedge we heard
Children shouting at their play,
The weekend hammers and mowers.

&

We were reading *Vanity Fair.*
I thought she'd fallen asleep,
As she often did, both bony hands
Clasped on the ebony cane,
While we sat there in her study.
I stayed watching her
Until first light surprised me.

I made her a coffin of maple
From boards I prised out of the floor
In the ballroom, where no one
Danced as long as I'd been there.
Then I made her a grave,
Not deep, on the croquet lawn.
I was in her service
One week short of thirty years.

I learned a seventh skill
Carving her name on the hearthstone
I levered from the study
And hauled from the house on a sled.
Just her name, and the year she died.
I knew none of the other details.

Owen at Play

Ex nihilo, Owen imagines, then contrives,
A world where he's the sole intelligence.
From Tinkertoy parts inert on the bedroom floor
He fuses wooden stars into galaxies.
In his own good time these spiky suns
Will implode into characters—one-eyed, spiny, good
And bad—shoved about all their lives by huge
Incomprehensible grubby hands. They divine
Meaning in their lives only as seething breath,
Some celestial sheriff in his fury,
From whose own clumsiness both good and bad
May earn a beheading or dismemberment;
Or when he is merciful, oblivion.

That whisper's a portent: whom he would destroy
He renders helpless first with pricks and smarts.
Next, discord. Then anguish and terror spread
Indiscriminate through the frail universe.
Behold, not one bright block on another! Lo,
The *Realpolitik* of the Crackerjack animal circus!
Weep for the fingerpuppet, crammed before
Its time in a jigsaw box, whose pieces have long
Dispersed like Bikini atoms, God only knows where.

Wouldn't the Mother of God herself cry out
To him to cease and desist from this wrathful harvest?
Inscrutable lawgiver, turn from your terrible labour!
Put off the Apocalypse! Bestow on this chaos
The order only you can perceive, and leave
The world to sleep in your sabbatical peace.

The Picture of Little Rory in a Municipal Park
Saxe Point, Victoria, BC., January 1975

Weary Rory dawdles on the path
Beneath the cedars where the light is dim,
As in ancestral caves. A bramble tugs
His sleeve, his face pale in the green shade,
Flanked by shards of fern, embraced by thorns—
Unlikely alabaster cherub in the wild
Greenery of a Douanier Rousseau—
He's no more my child than anyone's. Behind him,
A massive boulder looms, the tumbled head
Of a crude colossus, hewn by the torpid ice
A million years ago.
                              I've turned, prepared
To call *Hurry up!*—But again I'm in the wrong
Place for fathers, under these boughs reduced
To a superfluous attendant. Now the light
Is fading quickly, threatening more snow,
And I've lost perspective. Rory, motionless
This moment in the whispering palace of cedars,
Is untimely pensive, as Velasquez made
His Infanta in the scene where dog and dwarf,
Attendant maid, the artist himself, are all
Stopped by a premonition in a room
As dark as the grove we're halted in. I'll call
Across this little distance, and he'll come,
Slow as ice, footprint in melting snow
Small as a bird's, and beg to be carried home.

Astronomy

These nerves, these nebulae,
Filter a thin light
Years in all directions.
All cluttered creation looms.
God, anonymous as frost,
Relaxes over innumerable
Dissolving galaxies.

My head, this wrinkled planet,
Keeps emitting a garbled message.
Cells die, disappear, in the other
Galaxies: Abdomen, Wrist,
Larynx, Aorta, Eyelid,
And lonely remote little Penis.
God stretches, yawns, turns His back.
Black holes drink the stars where He was.

Death of Fathers
for Ken McCullough

His plane exploded
In oily black and red
On the Persian desert:
The dusty crescent of mountains
Wheeling at the edge of vision;
The tawny ground veering up.
I felt it behind other dreams,
Waking up sweating and shaking,
To stare at myself while I shaved,
Slow to focus on my own face.

Every detail severely familiar:
The instruments warping and cracking,
The roar of flame in the cockpit;
His stern frown, one arm raised
To see better, unbelieving;
The ground reeling up through the glass—

What reason have I to believe
He died as he wanted to?

My mother took to the madhouse;
His mistress knelt discreetly
At the back of the church for the service.
My uncles, my brother and I
Brought the coffin with ashes
Gathered from the desert
To the family grave. It was all
Acted out with the proper restraint.

I'm cold enough now to let
This elegy rise between us.
All that time, every detail
Has stayed as clear as a curlew's
Call in the night: he still
Grips the useless controls.
The unchanged ground spins up.

Requiem for my Mother
Maureen McAuley, 1906-1969

In the memory of the dead
Is the consolation of the living

MOURNERS

The widow returns to the house
And accepts the quiet room,
The polished furniture.
Her hands rest in her lap.
She will soon find something to do
With her hands again. She says
His name aloud in the room.

&

The one whose shoulder aches
From the weight of his sister's coffin
Has turned his back to the wind
To light a cigarette.
Flame hollows his skull;
Wind rips the smoke from his hands.

&

The man whose wife is lying
Between the four tall candles
Waits for the women to leave,
Then climbs the stairs again
To quench the candles, one
By one. Then he sits all night
In the dark room beside her.

For the grieving are as numerous as the blades
Of the long reeds that bend in every wind,
Surviving, though their hollow roots hold sand.
As sorrow leaves us, so wind dies in the reeds.

"ALLE HERRLICHKEIT DES MENCHEN"
God of my childhood
Set free these dead
From the chains of my prayers

God of the light
That fixes this dead
Shadow at my heel
Make me in wisdom
Set free these dead
At last from my grief.

VIGIL
In my town the old sea-captain
Whose skin was sailcloth, whose speech
Was a gusty spittle, whose lies
Were crimson anemones that swayed
In the blue rockpools around
The sea-green edge of my town—

In my town the captain was last
From his wrecked ship in a roaring
November storm—the breeches-buoy
Lifting him like a saint
Assumed into heaven over the rocks,
The breakers, and up the cliff
To the room with dim prints of ships
In full sail, where his pipe
Wheezed while he told me great lies.

In my town, at the rosary
The night they coffined him,
He was only another
Wheyfaced pensioner
Already gone straight to heaven
With the reek of Murray's Plug
Tobacco for a halo.
This was the first I'd seen
Of him with his weather eye closed.

GLORY

I sifted the coarse yellow sand
Through the hollow of my fist.
My heels dug inches in sand.
I bit on a reed from the dune
Where our loving had left its mark.
I tasted its salt. I made
Coarse music with it, a rasp:
The corncrake's misleading call.

The girl with me held wide
Her towel to show me her dark
Nipples, her shadowy pubes,
And covered herself again quickly.
Her laughter and my cry
Of shame and delight were flung
On the light wind over the bay.

Oh survivors, who among you
Will grieve with me for those voices
Which die away in the whisper
Of small waves and the birds' piping?

SURVIVORS

Chaplain:
Four shells on four yards
Of trench in the stripped wood
The Somme   July 1916
O horrible   most horrible
Trapped him in a dugout
With three fusiliers who cursed
Their bad luck first, but prayed
With him later, panting,
Words a flat hiss on poison air.

The next barrage tore bright strips
From their eyes: the sky opened
Over the foul death-trench.
In gaseous day, in the childish
Whines of the unseen wounded,
They joked about the priest's hair
Turned white by that four-hour burial.

After the hospital morphine
They sent him to teach boys
Mathematics and History
Far behind the lines.
They let him grow dahlias and banks
Of rhododendron in the rich loam
Of the school's Pleasure Garden.
The boys called him Thatch or Shakes
Behind his back; but they liked it
When he took them to help in his garden.

Bombardier:
The youth who took
An ack-ack shard

Below the ribs
Was so fixed on
His bombsight that
He felt only a slight
Loosening

The plane kicked up
And banked for home
And he leaned away
From the silver threads
Of the railyard in
The crosshairs

Bombs away! he
Yelled and reached
For a cigarette
Into the bowels
That filled his flight
Jacket   he
Laughed and called
To the navigator
LOOK but the other
Was faceless dead

They sewed him back
Together but he kept
Asking for his old
Buddy   his
Navigator

Skipper:
A cable winching boxes
Of mackerel out of the hold
Snapped and tore both thighs.
In the Harbour Bar he drank

From their bottle of pre-war cognac
While he waited for the doctor.

Castrate, and both legs lost,
He sold his brother the trawler
For half its worth. He wrote
On the back of a factor's docket:
God has laid his curse
Now I am half a man.

In a black storm, his brother
Ran the trawler on Shenick Rocks.
The hull tore open like new bread.
His brother drowned; the crew
Brought off safe by the lifeboat.
For hours he shouted his brother's name
Into the flying spume, the luminous waves.

For everywhere with their comrades are heroes who dare
To carry their grief as Achilles bore his shield,
With Patrocles lost, into the maddening war.
Sorrow is with them everywhere, the shadow at the heel.

CREED

The rocks here, if they sang,
Would chant *Affirm! Affirm!*
They pile down from the cliff,
A great choir petrified
In the act of singing the canticle's
Sublime chord, *Amen!*
From the clifftop a summer forest
Spreads a green infinity
To meet the infinite blue
Of the sky that commands, *Affirm!*
But the cell that set my hand
To trembling while I wrote

Lets go, and dies. I wait
For the shadow below the cliff
To bury the choir of spilled rocks.

Then having, for this scene,
Invented the sun's death,
I kneel in the wild grass
With nothing to deny.

LABOUR AND TRIBULATION

Flattening dough for pastry,
Thumping the high kitchen table,
My mother's forearms swelled
Like a bosun's. She hummed
Her girlhood tunes—"Love's Old Sweet Song,"
"The Long, Long Road A-Winding"—
Every surface, all odours charmed
To attend her rare good humour.

Her hair was white at thirty.
My aunt (her advisor, though younger,
And pretty, and always in trouble
Over men) would sit with her drinking,
A bottle of Power's between them,
On wet Sunday afternoons.
They worried about money, family.
Their voices would bring me from reading
To the room where they changed the subject.

Soon from her hospital bed
She was scolding me: *Mind
Yourself, now.* In north-city
Slang, we joked about
Half-forgotten troubles
With pawnbrokers and bailiffs

And we so respectable!—
But she couldn't laugh as she used to,
Rocked by a giddy croaking—
One lung and part of the other
Gone: the family disease.

Not long after that we fought
Over money and didn't speak
For years. Then I wrote from the States
And signed my childhood nickname.
Soon she was dead from the whiskey
And pills and time to worry
About money and illness, and about
Her thankless children, I suppose.

God of light and shadow,
Let her rest in my understanding.

SECRET
What light painted
The ceiling with
Its map of cracks
And charted my path
Of sin and fear?
                    First light.

What age was I
When I could make out
The Devil's wing
In the cracked plaster
Over my bed?
                    The age of Unreason.

What sin occurred
While I was snug
In the warm bed
And my mother there
Warm in the dark?
No sin, no sin.

What fear tore through me when I planted
A row of green seedlings in my father's garden
As he directed? What fear when they shrivelled,
Killed by late frost?
The fear of venture
In a world of loss.

God of this new day
Set me free in your light
From this vain grief.

BLESSING

I will walk out today;
I will accept the shadow
Light casts for company.

I will walk out today,
Dry leaves, dry grass untroubled
By the shadow at my heel.

I will walk out today
With my children through the shadows
Of the wintry park.

They will play at hunting and hiding.
And when they grieve my going
This memory will bless them.

House Burning Down

What fire feeds on is mostly air, but I dwell
On what I own, how bitterly I'd start over.
Flame leafs through a shelf of books in minutes;
The pages swell into rippling levels of yellow.

Hoses curl from the engines to the men
Who lean back from the seething jets, the glare
On their faces like saints beholding a vision.

The busy lapping inside that unfixed roar
Holds to a staunch pattern. I draw closer
Through my fear. If only I could command
Fire, the oldest language, our mother tongue!

Now books and shelf are one. Flame sheathes
The roofbeam. To a great shout of timbers, the house
Leans inward. The doorway conjures a seamless
Red-orange-grey curtain for the vanishing rooms.
Fire smiles in the teeth of a cellar window,
Then pours a firmament of sparks into the sky.

Flames chatter to each other, a fierce lingo.
I turn my back to recall the names of objects
Liquified by flame: *book, lamp, table, chair.*

And on my way home I call a blessing
On every sleeping house against the black
Ashes after the yellow flames depart.

Take Up Thy Bed
—John, 5:8

My earliest memory? Why, the lassitude!
The servant's spoon at my mouth, the long
Staring at my feet, the crude charts they made
From their coverings, the stains relating where
I went and could not go....The cutting reek
Of old piss, the dung-reek of my own bed—
My thighs scratching together when they carried me
Through the city to the waters I had no faith in.

My father in his prime died of the plague,
Howling his soul's curse at the marble walls.
They tell me his name is in the chronicles,
For his reforms after the wars. At thirty-seven
I inherited the cursed villa, and the green balm
Of its gardens, and his salaaming servants. Found
No treasure, though everyone said we were rich.

The sickness had by then drawn greyish skin
Tight to the bones of my arms and legs. The stench
Of a cow's belly cut open, of spewed offal, rose
From me while I lolled on satin and dreamed
The indolent movement of others swaying around me.

My servants feared the spirit of my father.
For a year or so, until they began to forget
His power, they fetched me down to the pool. Useless!
What a figure I must have cut in my silk swaddlings,
My head full of ideas, impressions...the pillow
Wearing the hair from the nape; my features a child's
Leathern mask for the game of 'Beggars'. What
A spectacle we made at the pool, my Egyptians
Lifting me naked into the bubbling mire!

Free for a while afterward from my own stench,
I could lie in the garden, steeped in ribald birdsong,
And burst a grape on my palate with my tongue;
Numbness on numbness, yet the sweet grape burst,
And its juice filled my throat while old Lares told
His tales of champions on horseback with spear
And shield, doing battle for the Pharoah
And his Princess. He related the clamour and flash
Of events as strong for the brain
As the grape bursting in my mouth.

But old Lares with the rest forgot in time
My father's spirit pacing the echoing rooms.
I woke one morning, sunlight full on my bed,
So bright that the painted figures on the wall,
The plump daemonic dancers, seemed to cavort
Alive in the ritual grove. Silence. The air
Waited to tremble with pipes, and naked feet
Drumming on naked earth. My four senses
Tortured me with this silence. They had fled
At last, and stolen even the sacred lamps
From the altars. What fear must have gone with them!
Why had they waited so long? And yet, how timely!

Three silent days. Then a gang of slaves,
Freed by age or disease from their masters, crept
Through the villa like spiders. They found me swathed
In lambswool and satin, so thirsty I couldn't talk,
Except in a hoarse grunt. This way I pleaded all day;
And after dark, the two strongest carried me down
To the Street of the Angel's Pool, where I could beg
For scraps and live with the other beggars.

A child of ten, no more,
Sores on arms and legs,
Stuffed hard crusts in my mouth.
She watched my tongue as an owl
Watches the young in her nest.
I choked down the rough crumbs.
Straw for a bed, like the beasts.
A long dying, before the miracle.

To feel at my heel the smooth stones,
The slime on the walls, the oily waters
Breaking brown on my brown skin—how strange!
The coarse cloth between my fingers, the scabs
On old sores, the dizzy business of standing—
Strange! Pain clambers along this tree
Of nerves that nods queerly at the body's news—

Tongue clatters its new consonants
As grapes would burst against my teeth. I hold
Another, limp, greyskinned, genderless,
In my arms as my slaves held me, and I lower him
Into the waters. He has hope....How soon
My whole being grows into these new movements!

Recital

There's a certain way to do this, right or wrong.
Crossing your legs can be a matter of taste.
Plenty of seats in front—but watch your tongue!

Who listens to a naked woman's song?
Playing Brahms or Verdi, do you feel chaste?
There are certain ways to do this, right or wrong.

The metronome, the tuning fork's keen prong—
Nothing you practise with passion is a waste.
Plenty of seats in front—but hold your tongue!

Don't assume your beloved knows how long
It has been since you first sat down and faced
The certain way to do this, right or wrong.

And Petrarch, in the chapel at Avignon:
Could he have seen Laura praying while she graced
The *prie-dieu* in front of him, and held *his* tongue?

There's plain water to drink at every feast,
And jewels adorn, whether real diamonds or paste.
How you feel is neither right nor wrong.
Plenty of seats in front, if you hold your tongue!

The Exile's Book of Hours (1982)

The Exile's Book of Hours

Prelude In Darkness

Veni, Deus. Old ideas, like stairs,
Climb between me and a clear concept
Of the divine: I wait for a call
I fear won't come. Nothing personal,
Marcus Aurelius, but what's left
Is no more than the split hairs

Between the unknowable Absolute
And the mannish divinity
You Ancients lent to marble.
In our time, it is comparable
To a clear connection between, say,
Detroit and Dresden. You know the fruit

Of prayer is a mouthful of dry seeds.
Those moments devoted to saying over
Worn phrases, fingering smooth beads,
Dismal litanies of our daily needs,
Could be given to, say, praising a lover
While you helped her into her coat. Creeds

Are ramparts Reason has raised
Out of the slop and dross
Of unspoken feeling. *Can we get on,
Your Holiness?* Ego rasps: then
Strings and brass aspire. The chorus, uncertain,
Then sings praise.

SHORT JOURNEYS BEFORE DAYBREAK

I am the amber-eyed black
Cat who forsakes her species
To curl in the widow's lap.

I am jackal: can change places
With any beast of the griping
Night-chorus. I am colourless, faceless.

I am mollusc: without will, gaping,
I wait for the sea, my lover,
To change me, a soft gasping.

I am hawk. A speckling moves. I hover,
Dive. A thin scream escapes.
I strike and strike. Will this end? Never.

I am bear, wrestling clumsily with my hopes.
Sleep is my oldest friend; I have one other.
When resentment straightens me into a corpse,
I lie with the Prince of Lies: man, stepbrother.

DAYBREAK

Newstime! Rise! Shine! Shake a leg!
Neuroses, Nemesis, Behold! I bring
TV tidings! What's a fad? What's a drag?
Outrage over coffee, of thee I sing—
Sex fiends, bigots, cartels, murderous falange—
My lungs boil, my guts fret for revenge.

Vanity, old deathshead friend, old bore,
Comes to chat while I shave and shiver.

A masque ensues, behind the fogged mirror.
I want, offstage voice announces. *Chancer,*
Who d'you think you are? Comes Ego's answer.
This can go on all day, hour after hour.

Contrast: Black ellipses
Spread in soft new snow:
My children's path to school.
New light, a gold mist, blesses
Their going. Such moments, so few,
I take to heart, God's own fool.

EARLY MORNING WALK TO WORK

Turn off the boob tube, take an ulcer pill.
Brouhaha! The sun is over the hill,
The cat is cleaning his fur on the warm sill.
Sing *Brouhaha!* Turbulent, damnable Will!

Go, my soul, patrol the patio
Between the theatre and the studio
Where speech and clay, player and potter prepare
To give the word its flesh, palpate mute air.
What news? What news? Tell me, Horatio.

LATE MORNING TALK
  My Students Refuse The Craft

Away   away   this allure
        this yearning East   *appassionato*
inevitably takes you
        (our fond joke)   over

The unseen line   the *taboo*
       whatever way you turn   however
yearning   you feel the Self burn
          down to zero
desire   you cannot spurn
       gravity in one clap
rolling the flat map
       up   into a globe

Passing all   understanding   a lobe
       of sand   a tropic   latitude
surrendering   its name   Gratitude

Now   whatever course   is drawn
       west is true   already known
you are free   go   the same
       invisible way   every island   artless
          lying   prone
ocean steppingstones   on your charts
       all the blue   way home

NOON APOCHRYPHA

In the forenoon I rose up
       & went into hiding from my Life.
In the Midst of Heavy Routine,
       Whilst I partook of Coffee & a Smoke,
It was borne in upon me
       How vain & futile the whole Thing was.
My Guts were aflame in their Acids
       & my Brows they burned with Insomnia.
For mine Enemies have encamped about my sore Brains.
Ai, my five Sons all in a bad Dream
       Have been estranged of me,

Following hard upon the Departures of their Mothers,
Who, in their several divorced Tongues
          Have cursed me,
And lamented in a Chorus
          Their Unhappiness with me,
Though I have betaken my Self
          Unto a Lifetime of Striving for their Sakes.

Yea, have I laboured to placate these inconsolable Women,
In Tribulation & Turmoil,
          All for five Minutes' Affection:
The purblind hasty Rutting
          On the quaking Bed; the ammoniac Reek;
The oystery levelling Lovemuscle;
          The bleak Sheets
That after such Sessions of hard Bargaining
          Bore my Signature.

For I am weary of my Life
          & would fain walk from it,
Or rise from this aching Dream,
          Or sink into dreamless Sleep,
Yea, even at Day's noon Height.

Meditations of Afternoon

          De Mortuis...
Is it good in broad daylight to reflect on death?
The tricked brain's fused circuits, despair's stale breath—
Who can grasp the particulars? For example,
The young poet who sank from his gun, from a simple
Surfeit of powers—what generous, tender psalm
Evoked, but could not reveal, death's mysteries?
He wrote of his boyhood on the levee, becalmed

In sunlight. I recall a summer's ebbtide beach:
Shells gleam, strange tokens of a power beyond reach.
Neither his death, nor the slight catastrophes
Of my slow going, counts for more on the globe
Than, for example, the gnat caught in the trembling web.

INTERLUDE, WITH ALTER EGO

Waxwing gather along thin phone wire:
Notes from an unfinished score.

Sing, ye choruses, sing out
Upon late sunlight's sloping glare.

Sing, soulmate soloist, silvervoice!
Had I your gift, your delicate air,

I'd raise the spirit from its mire of doubt,
Singing *Alleluia!* chanting *Rejoice!*

CATNAP, WITH NIGHTMARE

What comes here? Splenetic
Accursed old Ego, never
Satisfied, vaults and tumbles
From behind drawn stagecurtains
(Pink-and-gold brocade, embroidered
With masks and timbrels). Upright,
He grins and feints, urgent, tough
(Proscenium arch of plaster
With garlands and grinning sylphs),
Gestures, exhorts, then insults
In Russian or Kurdish. I lean

Forward to catch the meaning.
But the conductor has raised
Big stubby hands
Over the hidden orchestra
(Trumpets, cymbals, a fierce drumming)
And Ego, bent at the waist,
Mutters ingratiatingly.
Agued and stern, he holds
His cropped head (clap hand,
Clap hand, till silence comes home).

LATE AFTERNOON, RUNNING:
CLOSE REASONING, LISTENING CLOSELY

Lift me, God, from the Self's diurnal fussing,
That I may see the futility of paper,
The nagging transience of plan and project,
The insensate beggary of every object
I cling to: show me each in true and proper
Relation—though I feel I may be addressing

You, God of this blank white world, as an abstraction.
Some say you are Nature, and Law is your reflection;
Others disparage, murmuring you are Absolute
Zero, cosmic comedian. Other beliefs are too rash,
Even for me, too finite; though, irresolute,
I long for One who gives clay life, words flesh.

Infinite God, I pray in the terrible glimmer
Of your perfection, what is your secret will?
Like King Claudius, I feel faith grow dimmer,
Heavier with the world's weight: I could fulfil
Yet a stratagem, claim a small victory....
Lift me up, God, into your mystery!

SUNSET

My children make their way home,
Dragging their feet through the snow.
A robin lets one note fall
Through muted air. God, how can I know
You? Light retreats. The cold hour has come
For surrender. Why should it ravel

My every sense to mouth this word? To call
Above the clamour of the will to some
Mighty impression of you, sacred foe
Whose image we design and limn and frame
After our own—and with such brazen skill
We claim an intimacy, bathe in the afterglow

Of your immense absence. God, I grow
Weary of guess, and would yield all
The ground I hold against the mortal claim
You make on me, if you would once reveal
Yourself with a clear sign. Then I would go
On my knees repeating your right name

In prayer, and you would be as a footfall
Leaving its dark impression on the snow,
Leading me the true way home.

from *Coming & Going* (1989)

The Nun of St. Michan's

for Joanne and Rubén Trejo

Among the bodies preserved in the crypt under St. Michan's
Church, Dublin, is that of a thirteenth-century nun, aged about
twenty-four at her death.

This, this is God's will.
I repose in my narrow box
Of cracked deal, my head turned
Aside this way, not from shame,
Though my poor brown shroud
Long ago shredded to dust, and you,
Pilgrim, who climb down
Where the dry air keeps our bodies
Without corruption, can see
This portal of bone and coppery
Skin which caused me great shame
While I strove to keep my vows
And live by God's will.

On the morning I was made
A chaste Saviour's Bride,
They cut away the child's
Few fair locks from my head
And dressed me so no mortal man
Would tempt me, or be tempted.
Prostrate on the flagstones
At the altar in my white surplice,
I surrendered all my worldly
Powers, and vowed to obey
The Abbess's rule, and to keep my body
A pure gem for Mary's crown,
Intacta; to own nothing, but to give
My labour in penance for the world's sins.
Then I put on the coarse brown
Garment that would be my shroud,

And joined our little company.
We chanted God's praise at all hours,
In the glow of many candles, willing
Captives of the Holy Spirit.

But soon my own body betrayed me—
A black spasm of torture and release—and sleep,
O sleep brushed my face with his wing,
My hands fluttered like wings,
I wept that Christ my Bridegroom
Would not forgive my wickedness
And drive him away from me, this demon
Who chuckled and snored in the throats
Of my sisters as they lay in their cots!

Between labour and prayer
In our little chapel, silence.
I tried, as my confessor
Bade me, to look on the Cross,
To contemplate His wounds,
His blood our healing wine,
His body our bread of grace.
But often half swooning I dreamt
Of Him borne down to me
As any bride would have it.
How was this God's will?
Prayer perished on my lips.
Then the day's round in expiation
For past sins; for sins
I knew I would yield to.

On my knees where I scrubbed the kitchen hearth,
In the field where I sheaved the meagre wheat,
On the bog where I bore the baskets of turf
For the fires, I begged to be rid of this flesh
That would corrupt all my thought. But God

Answered no prayer of mine. Christ died
For my sins, but would not redeem me—So
As His widow in my coarse smock and shawl
I knelt in the mud by the Liffey and thumbed out
The few roots to flavour our meal. It seemed

Scarcely a moment after my eyes closed
On the dizzy water, the clouds in an uproar,
That I heard my sisters chirping like mice
And I so cold, and the bog's fragrances,
And strange grunted prayer as they carried me
Back to my cell. Was it all a dream, those years,
Psalms, beeswax, rosaries, the sins of my flesh,
Stroke upon stroke of the switchbroom over
The convent floors, until that sinking down
To lie stretched full by the river in surrender?

Because the power of flesh
Could waken me into wedlock
With Christ's bodily form
As I contemplated His Cross,
And God answered no prayer of mine,
I turned my head aside
With my last strength when the Abbess
And her priest urged me to kiss
His crucified flesh. Then breath
Left me at last to this quiet,
This brown unaging stillness,
Intacta. This is God's will.

Coming & Going

Look, how we curl into sleep after love:
Our bodies are so content, they convey
No more sense than a pair of gourds
In a Cézanne *Nature mort,* or a tableau
Of Beckett's—when a brushstroke or a sigh
Allows for shapes that may not have been there.

In this way our spirits have climbed out
To stroll the Cerulean, where
Time and space are one. While form
Is a mere memory, our souls

Dance, those sleeping husks so far
Removed that being without matter makes
Clear sense.
     Now light attends
The window, to give flesh its due.
Thigh at hip and head on breast, we wake.
And when that dance plays out, we'll take
Our ease in heaven, just like this.

The Dying Swan

The piano ripples a delicate
Evocation of water; then the hands
Of the cellist, in the light
From the music-stand, form at the wrists
Into opposed heads, a kind of puppetry
Required to derive a *frisson* of mourning
From the instrument's long throat—and that figure,
Slight as mercury in its glass vein,
The weather's wisdom—a girl, a being in white,
Confined between the planes of floor,
Blue backdrop, and wings—conveys
Death's flight by winnowing her wrists....
And we reflect on swans, on waters where they die
Into eternal blue. The girl lowers
Her feathered head to her white breast,
Opens a lifeless hand, and the light leaves her.
Afterward for hours the breath of meaning
Stirs the painted veils that memory
Has made of the dance and the cello's lament.
The movement of these figures throws a shadow
We take for truth, though it be no more than the swan-
Shadow anyone can make by pursing the fingers
And bending the wrist as you would to draw the bow
Across the strings—if you can find a white backdrop,
And put yourself between it and the light, and feel
The swan's weather in the carotid.

Aor Against the Warmonger

Look at the hands, kept out
From the sides, to draw his guns
On cue for thousands of takes
In those cowboy stand-offs.
He could still play bit parts
In black-and-white campaigns
Where his side won every time.

He should groan without cease
From the small ancient pains that live
In his bowels; but he'd shrivel
Into a leathery foetus before he'd admit
To fear. He finds this code of use also
When marines die in their barracks,
One of the many fatal mistakes he lived through.

Look at him, hair a black cowl, as odd
As a bishop's mitre or a dowager's
Tiara, his tireless tongue
Chewing on those hoary lines—
This creature, this incomplete
Reptile awaiting fulfillment
In the wreckage of Eden. He'll keep
Coming back to life until he finds
A world befitting him. Picture

A sandy islet, the cobalt tropics.
The salty reek of shellfish. Wrinkled neck
Thrust out, head sideways, the aged iguana
Manoeuvres stiffly, blunt horny toes
Pushing through his own dung.
He lurches heavily forward, the forked

Tongue darting. Shrill seabirds
Dive on him. Maggots and lice
Rummage in the cracked rubbery skin.

This is the world war has given him.
This is the role we assign him,
To play this scene over and over
Until he understands and gets it right.

The Exile on his Failing Vision
Sandymount Strand, June 1982
i.m. JJ

I

Hup! I come to a halt, facing the sea. Count
Blessings. I can wait. In the holy hour I spent
Walking these tide-ribbed sands, my sight gave way
To something of the dazzling play between air
And matter, near and far, Howth and the bay,
Cloud and horizon, and the fugitive sun.

Light slanted down that wet sand, a benediction.
But the focussing muscles refused their function.
Sight had nowhere to go—could only skitter along
The sea's rim, jigging with sandpipers
And the little dancing waves of Sandymount.

Back the short stretch to our flat, I'm compelled
To go slow. Is this heart trouble? Wait.

II

Returned to desk and book, pad and pen, the eyes
Have their work cut out for them: clouds gallop
Over the page with a meaningless verve, like pups
Chasing their yapping shadows on the strand.

I concentrate, and try another page
Or two. I can wait. Words, words. What troops
Parade here, under what colours, pray?
Now comes a double image of a double image,
A shimmering misgiving, the print reduced
And edged by light. Sequence, consequence

Blink like stars; words glisten like cockleshells.
Sentences go past, waving, to the front;
Another paragraph pulls alongside; docks.

Consonants march out, two abreast. Hail, vowels!
A new page surrenders its odours of damp
Pulpwood and machine oil. The other senses,
They say, learn to serve better. I can wait.
Stars break under the eyelids. *His milde Yoak.*

III

The overgrown roses have speckled the granite sill
With crimson petals. Evening has taken all
But the topmost branches of the great sycamore.
Small clouds drift out to sea—a handful of petals
Thrown on a purple cloth. All heaven's treasure.

A pool on the strand this moment is as deep
As the advancing tide will let it be. Light waits
In its retina. The curlew's heartbreaking call.
A dog splashes through, and the pool breaks
Into countless crystalline stars. The eye rescues
This image, remembering in its darkness

Youth could neither escape nor understand
Such play between impossible and possible.

Three Acts from a Play

I

For one season, much laughter: we learned to take
In our stride the age's age-old joke,
What we most desire, we must let go.
On the crucial evening, I sat through a show
While she sailed off, resolved, it seemed, to mend
What matters needed mending with her friend.
She trimmed her jib, though: leaving the theatre
I found her, radiant as a changed character
Who remembers with delight the earlier scene
Which made change possible, with all its pain.

II

She opened the lower button of her blouse,
Pausing at a mirror as we left the house.
"Temptress!" I called to her, as though in prayer.
"Not so," she said. "What, then?" "A woman's power."
Then, to divert me from that truth, she laughed.
But her perfume, at its body-temperature, left
No doubt she could rouse the four winds from their rest,
Or start the hero on his journey west.
"You explain all history," I replied.
Ever since, she's contentedly denied
She meant more by it than her smile. She must know,
By leaving that lower button open, how
She could command, from lover or passerby,
After surrender, lifelong loyalty.

III

Her womanhood collected into a pale
Version of herself waking up, a smile
Half-composed on her lips, as though to right
A wrong or heal the sick. "More light," I thought,

And flooded the room with it, to photograph
"The Lady Waking"—but she disturbed with a laugh
That pallor, that balanced moment, desire
Ready to be fulfilled. And now, make-up on, the hair
Fashionably combed, she may go serene
Among strangers and friends, none of whom have seen
Child, girl, woman, all at once—
The spirit waking to our world of sense.

from
Meditations, with Distractions (2001)

A Farewell to His Poems

Go, little gnats, little clever jackdaws, take
Off, you overdressed parrots, get out of my sight,
Not another word, with your coughs and hiccups,
Signals to your accomplices—after all
Those checks and corrections—go on, get what
You can while you can. You weren't meant

To turn out this way. I had in mind a play
Of light and sense, a dance, a leap, but demons
Possessed you as you took shape. Don't blame
Me when you go out in the world as runts,
As stammering badgers. How could I raise
Such a brood of foundlings, buzzing and prattling
And squabbling under my roof, and send you off
In style, trim, well-spoken, mannerly?

Well, go now. I won't regret the mouths I had
To feed so I could get you on your way, if you
Can bring a moment's pause to one foe, one careerist,
One crawthumping bigwig hypocrite. Only a father
Could love you, my poppets, my treasures, hostages
To many a dark and doubtful hour. Go, you're free,
You changelings, to live on your wits, to leave me
Like this and take all I have—go where you must—
But never let on you're mine.

A Shift in the Wind
for Dave & Beth Britt

We keep heaving forward, but the shifty wind
Begins to jig in the mainsail, flapping it happily,
Tilting it over and round on our own wake,
And the leeward gunwale sinks into seething foam,
And the jib empties and ripples and we lose
Speed. The hand on the tiller wants to push
Angrily round off the wind; we'd lug and yar,
Reel and keel downwind to a slithering standstill
Like a sternstopped plough in its furrow. But you reach
To release the mainsail, jam over the rudder, and we jibe
Like an elegant drunk at a wedding dance, giddily
Balanced on the liquid floor, waltzing that woman,
That fickle Old Lady, whose presence we know
From the sail's belly filling, her laughter in the rigging.
We cinch all the lines, lean back and let her go.

From Hospital (an unfinished sequence)

WAITING ROOM

Pursuant to their respective professions,
God, Death, the Devil, and St. Jude
Were sitting around in the Waiting Room, late one night.

"God is good," God said, not letting on
Who he was. The Devil smiled
At him in sympathy.

"Great and good and merciful," St. Jude
Added, without looking
At anyone in particular.

The Devil smiled at St. Jude also.
"Indeed, indeed," he murmured.
Death got up and left the room

And went to the third floor to take
The infant who, they said, was out of danger;
And to the fifth floor, and put

The old Indian out of his misery;
And to the O.R., to put a stop
To the brain-dead biker's revival.

He left the evangelist comatose
In the I.C.U., and rejoined the others,
Who were reading old issues of *Time*

And drinking coffee not fit
For human consumption. He addressed
God first, explaining the biker's innocence.

To Jude he made a special plea,
For the plight of the old Indian, a pagan,
Weighed on his conscience. To the Devil

He said, "Lucifer, God's own fool, the child
Is yours." The Devil complained, "Ah, now,
What would I want with a child? The biker'd be

More in my line." God, still believing
He was *incognito,* frowned and raised
A pointing finger. "God will decide. You know

Not the day nor the hour." St. Jude, who knows
The odds against everyone and picks the long shots,
Went over on that account to take

Death's skinny hand in his own plump fist
And blabber gratefully, "As long as even
One of these can be saved from doom

By a miracle with my name on it,
My job here's worth the trouble."
He wasn't sure what official part

Death played. God rolled his eyes to heaven.
"Wait now," the Devil fumed, "I'm the joker
In this pack. Take back the baby and play

By the rules. I'll wait for the evangelist
To croak." "Ask God," said Death, "He's here too."
"Damn it," God protested, "you've no right.

"I'll reveal myself when the time comes."
Death did not stay to argue,
But went again on his rounds.

THE SACRAMENT OF THE TABLETS
for Rubén Trejo

On the ceiling of the Temple of Oblivion
A scrolled proclamation admonished, *"Rise!"*
And a shadow drew aside his veil of sleep.
Duly he rose. Upon the incensed air
That held his torso upright for the rituals,
It was borne in upon him that he should accept
The will of the priestess leaning over him.
He held his right palm level out and there
Discerned a slight weight when she pressed the two
Tablets, intoning sacred mantras: *Take these*
For pain, and drink. Take these, and sleep.
After her benediction—*There, now*—he lay back
Into sheets of clouds and, a saint astray,
Drifted through temple precincts until he came
To a hall hung with filmy membrane, rose and pearl,
And he started humming, weightless, in the shell
Of light descending through the incensed air
From the ceiling in the Temple of Oblivion.

LIFEBIRD

An awkward thing this from nose to tail, a craft
As noisy and misshapen as a flying tadpole, designed
In the worst of taste as a magic windmill to lift
Straight up from Emergency and grind
The air from here to there to fetch back
Humpty-Dumpty from under his wall, or George
Away from his dragon. Now we're neck-and-neck
With a tragic ending as this one's eyes grow large
With a fast-forward story that passes understanding.
We take him down for the surgery as gently
As gravity will allow for a safe landing.

169

With the rotor's halo above him he must feel saintly,
If he feels at all, for he's getting ready to die,
The way he stares up from the stretcher, eyes all sky.

RECOVERY ROOM

Slip one breath
Into the next. Here
The only function's
Breathing. All in green
Goes my medico, one-
On-one with scope and chart,
Checking the vitals.

He's checking parts without
Feeling; also without the sense
To collect ethereal signals
That say, *Feel that. Feel that.*
Nerves intimate sickly
Routines, indecent business
With offal-whiff, fear-groans, slick
Eel-fingers in latex.

Who calls out these names?
Who thought up such names?
They mean great wounds, great
Afflictions. I steal away
Into unfeeling zones. Snap
Back into pain. Into great pain.

Attendants in green swaddlings
Steer their preoccupied gurneys
In and out of Nirvana.
Sooner or later, poor souls,
They get caught in body-traffic:

A chin tipped up from its neck
Like a foot without toes;
A clay-white foot on its heel:
Toes arranged on a chin.

Tongue works on sandy teeth.
But I've no wish to converse
With my neighbour, ghastly Elder
Supine to my right. He's
The keeper of death's dirty

Little secrets, by his looks; has put
Some distance between his old
Friend Pain and those *Vitals*
They keep checking on the charts.

An *ad hoc* committee forms
For a meeting in my head—
The only hideout left
For the delegates from all quarters
To deliver their reports.

We've passed a resolution
To keep quiet till we're rolled out,
One way or the other, before
We protest the conditions here
Between one breath and the next.

Cardiac Arrest

a white   room   was rising
or falling   hard   to tell
a ringing   below   or above
no way   to be   sure
above   a fine   white shell
or vault   a dome   ivory
or bone   from below
slight   palps   the spine
or skull   now   the ringing
has eased   whispering
a long   sigh

many   in one   we were drawn
down   a roaring   tunnel
or cloister   and rose   into white
light   or no light   a high gale
or   silence   glory

now you   thunderous
pump in my ear
you   call me   back
to your   numb   fears
the aches   that reach   back
you   your red   thumping
fills   the white   room

DELIVERY ROOMS

Mater:
He remembers nothing definite: images
Of crimson pleasure, a pulse like rain falling
Over a sea-sweep. After he was born
He kept nothing down, and in six weeks was given
Up for dead. "We had a little white
Coffin bought for you," his mother explained
Between whiskey-sips one cozy, dizzy evening
Two decades later, when tuberculosis
Had seized on both of them, and they were playing
"Down Memory Lane," that treacherous family game.

He imagines her in the Mater Hospital ward,
Herself a foetus, curled up and turned to the wall
So she wouldn't be made to leave the bed and see
Him dead in his cradle. She's foetal again now
In the wingback armchair, nursing a Baby Power's.
"That medical student was sure you were a goner,
So he gave you a thump in the chest, to kill or cure you."
She chuckles and leans to the fire with the poker
To riddle the coals. "Ah, the smile and the tear...."

Pater:
Fearing God, and much else besides
In a fancy nursing-home for rich neurotics,
His first wife—who'd blame her?—did three days
And nights of hard labour before a forceps tugged
Their firstborn into the April evening when all
They owned was on the never-never, not
A moment to lose between the final demand
And the overdraft. The son named after the father,
And the father's father, and his before him, for all
The good *that* did this eldest son, bless him.
She delivered their second quickly in Holles Street

173

And in the confusion lost her wedding ring.
Prayed to Saint Anthony and the ring turned up
In the bed under the baby boy who was given
The saint's name out of gratitude. Then they all
Went off to America, seeking a change in fortunes.

The third son named after Ireland's teenage martyr,
Kevin Barry, in a hospital far from the father
Who'd flown the coop which wasn't his scene since
He'd let his hair grow, drank too much, and split.
He should have gone back to them or been locked up,
And he deserved both. But it just wasn't his scene.
He drank at his ghosts, married again, moved on.

Familia:
Stern Owen, his fourth, blond and princely, he spied
Behind the hospital glass. Then he gladly announced
The birth at the Saddle Inn, his home-from-home.
Drinks for his friends. Drinks on the house. Drinks.

Soft and cheerful, Rory arrived in May
Of another year; basked by the back door
Or nuzzled his mother while the father thought,
In the manner of Berryman's mortal Henry,
Of how he could kill himself so nobody would notice,
So deep in loathèd Melancholy was he,
Also the heebie-jeebies and the dee-tees,
The rasp of memory, and his old pal Fear.
(It took some years to climb up to humility.)

Pace:
Fathers in overbright waiting-rooms, the nervous
Flicker of TV News and Sport, the bravado
And terror of three a.m., when the mothers are wheeled
Into rooms where they scream and moan and curse

174

At doctors and nurses like witches at their sabbath—
Pace, fathers. Sit. Stand. *Pace.* Wait for the news
From the rooms that Artemis long ago decreed
Were sacred to childbirth and men were banned.

Fathers feel in the throat the older growl
Of hunters on wild slopes, knives in their teeth—
Or is it the cigarette smoke they feel? Anyway,
Hunter and prey have vanished so long ago
There are few who sing those psalms and ballads now
To their children—half-forgotten tales
That once could summon *Creator Spiritus*
To house or hearth. Could he bring himself
To beg his children's pardon, make amends?

Someone has changed the channel. Salute, fathers,
Your mothers, and your children's mothers. Let
Your laughter be pleasing to the goddess, and amends
Will be made when the will is made to bend,
Now we're tuned to programmes where fathers may
Attend the birth of children and suffer the shame
Of being useless when they're needed most.

Spiritus Loci:
Terror's voltage shocked him head to foot
And blasted every law of life and death
While witless he witnessed, for forty hours and more,
His beloved in battle with his latest child,
Who wouldn't surrender to the fact of his birth
Till the surgeon caesared the womb and held
Him high at the forty-first eleventh hour.
Daniel his name, for a brave man we loved well.
Eyes clenched shut, he bleated angrily,
Not pleased with his parents who nevertheless
Managed a kind of awe, a kind of glee.

They let him carry this astonished son
To be weighed, labelled, and introduced to the world.
After the drug had released her into sleep,
He sat beside her bed and stared amazed and gave
Resentful thanks to the feckless *spiritus loci*
Of this and the other five delivery rooms.

DISCHARGE

Her voice is an octave above
The unbearable disinfectant
THIS EXPLAINS WHAT TO DO she yells
Right into my headache when you
Get home BE SURE BE SURE BE SURE
Four times a day with meals
Don't lift your weight if you feel
Or the other be sure to check
Sign here where it says signature
So YOU PAY YOU PAY YOU PAY
Or we take everything you have left
Take all your things with your things
Kidney-bowl mouthwash pills
FOR PAIN FOR PAIN FOR PAIN
This is the wheelchair to go
The distance from room four oh six
To the ground be sure not to
Walk till you can walk out
Without suing us
TAKE CARE NOW

The Sorrowful Mysteries

To the memory of my sister,
Anne Weldon, 1934-99

All I want, our mother would say,
Is peace, and turn away
From her canticle of grief
To change water and flour into a loaf.

Her muttering retreat, that house.
Her humours worked their leaven
Into waves of heat that rose
Round her at the oven.

Old songs and calamitous oaths
Were part of the daily office:
Jesus Mary and Joseph could be
A curse or a profession

Of shaken faith. For the rosary
Old Mary, her thick-and-thin friend,
Joined the giggling family.
When the whiskey was at its wits' end

And the cash and credit low,
Piety got its turn: prayer
Lifted her spirits from woe
And gave Christ back his share.

A Meditation, with Distractions
'Morgen'—Richard Strauss

A libidinous light flickers.
A trickle of trilling sound: a song-
Sparrow in the garden remembers
Arias from a well-favoured opera
And spills a phrase or two
Into the morning from the evergreens
Which defend the garden from the suburbs.
Now warming air plays on the brow;
The sparrow's lean piccolo gives way
To a radio voice, *O Lord,*
Deliver us, ever reminding us
Of Comedy's rueful promise
For the living and the dying which we all
Expect another to do for us
When the evil we need to be
Delivered from slips up on us
As we sleep or wake, snug or stuck
In some awkward scene or in
The brooder's miasma of light airs
And grace-notes rippling from the *arbor*
Vitae. Pianissimo. Langsam.

Comely chords and harmonies crowd into
The citadel the mind insists on making up
For the spirit's stillness, a whispering empire
No better than the dead grass and doghair
Of the sparrows' palaces in shadowy hedges
That sever neighbour from neighbour, light
From the mind locked in its battle with
The warriors of levelling lust, as in the Crusades
Prayers were hurled like spears, spears like prayers,

No matter what side God was on for the time being,
No longer deigning to play Redeemer—though *that*
Is yet a useful idea, a breath away
From making the right connection—

A screech. The kettle! Heaven's wrecked.
Towers, domes, steeples gurgle in the teapot.
Badly scratched ideas float in the headlines,
The lies, hungers, betrayals of the *Times*
Spread like marmalade on toast. I'm teased
By the prospect of Prospero's echo

Of Philomel's echo at Her Ladyship's
Dainty earlobe, whereto I bend my lips,
Having brought the tray to her bedside;
Hence to her clavicle's but a semi-colon.
Twenty centuries have passed
Between the ears before the teapot's scalded,
The toast buttered, the tray fondly arrayed.

Magus and Brahmin, dolt and dreamer—
All understand these distractions.

God's Pattern

Meditations on the Stations of the Cross,
with Distractions....

I Condemned

Hung there above
The nuns, you,
Red drops like darts
On your white outsides.

That frightened boy I was
Knelt in sin, clumsy
Street kid laced into
Boxing gloves to show off
The silly arts of self-
Defence to beaming mothers
At the convent drill display.
(Whose mother was too sick
To come? Whose d'you think,
Jackass?) Red drops, real blood,
On a white shirt when the round
Ended with the Angelus Bell
And rosary novenas on scraped knees
Benched before the thorn-crowned martyr-god.

Blood, blood, blood. The son
Tugged swathed in red
From the mother's womb
Soon learns cut-and-thrust
Wounds in a scrape with gang-boys

All along Church Street—gouts of it,
Streams, streaks, gouts of bloody offal
Over the slaughterhouse floor
Where we peeped in, straggling home
From bloody McGinty's bloody
Sixth Class National School.

II Scourge

Flesh. Flesh of the sweaty hand,
Flesh of calves and hams,
Flesh waltzing the path across from him,
That fag-dangling, mouth-agog youth I was,
Gaping after the Woman of the Town,
Flesh of round bubs and bum, Bridie.
For five quid, they said, she'd haul
His ashes for him—she'd tempt
That whipping snake to dance
Hilarious down his veins—

That sin-stained altar-boy I was,
Eager to be tormented more
By the wish for a whisk of a high warm wind
To strip Big Bridie of every stitch,
Reproduced in glossy *Mayfair* or *Men Only,*
Unholy magazines from dirty London
That found their way home
In unholy Father's flightbag.

III Cross

Vertical:
the sun's
bright side.
Vertigo reels the globe through
Its paces. Try to lift your head.
The crowd's
pulsed voice
draws you up
the cobbled
lane. Friends,
enemies,
urge you,
need you
erect here
to begin
the way

IV First Fall

To know yourself, *he said,*
And took me to my knees
With the weight of his lesson,
At your worst and best, *he said,*
Is to contemplate, *he said,*
This dirt, *he said,*
With your worm's eye, this
Humus you're made of, not
Whole, not sound enough
To be fearless face-to-face
With the dark loam,
Without friend or enemy.

V Mother

What laws, whose laws ordain
Your suffering when your son
Brings on himself this pain?
I could blame Miss Fortune,
The grizzled crone behind
The counter of her mean
Little sweetshop in Hand's Lane.
She robbed the children blind
And we robbed her to get our own
Back on the hucksters of the town,
Those greyfaced hoors, *Bless 'em all,*
The long an' the short an' the tall....

You must have told me often
I was forgiven, but I could hear
Only those rhymes to soften
The darkness you sang, the rare
Ineffable flight of your singing
The flesh and blood of my beginning.

The couplet on your gravestone
Had to wait until great wordstorms
Blew themselves out on the wall
Of my pitchcap stubborn skull
And death and I could come to terms
With all that's done and left undone.
Now from the prison of my will
You are released, so that your son
Lifts his own burden with his own arms.

VI Friend

A word from you   and you
Would lighten   what dark holds
Between   the bruised hills
My shoulders make   so I share
Your horizons   and the bleeding
Clouds   behind my back

But pardon   I don't make
Sense even   when you ask
For a simple   word of truth
Rather a rain   of blows
Than this   argument
Between self   and soul
O pardon   pardon   pardon

It is made   this plain   cross
Of words   I always   hear
From you   this fear   I can't help
You to end   this round   of words
It won't   close on   any sense
But which   tell me   which whips

Worse   the word   you help
Me with   or the long   agony
Between   horizons   of waking
In the spirit   or the body's   night?
Help me   now   the next
Step   pushes   under my feet

You   I have   long ago
Pardoned   you made   that easy
From   the very first   you who did
Me no wrong   take this   next step
With me   it is   so hard

VII Veronica

She who loves me is not loath,
When I battle to no avail
Lunging at that windmill death,
Trying to turn aside his flail.

She who keeps my mortal secret
Holds before me a veil of doubt.
Death turns to face me. She, in sacred
Blood has written my secret out.

I go forward a cruel step.
Cruelty follows close behind.
She whose love would ever keep
Me safe from death has left this sign.

Another step. I fail again.
Her veil is my mask of life
When death rounds on me again,
The seventh sense that feels love's knife.

VIII Second Fall

Simon says *Fall down*. Oh friend, don't come here
Where every pebble's a hill and weedy grass
Mimics a jungle cave where Prospero and Lear
Argue with Fate and nymph and satyr caress
Under a nettle's shade. To whatever gods are near,
Hidden behind the sky's grey veil, I confess
Unless you lift the skull-heavy load I haul
I may not rise again, though ants beckon, crickets call.

Brain. Membrane. Blood. Breath. Hindsight blinds,
Deafens me. The clever construct of skin, the ooze

Of venery, the wound of love open to the mind's
Fervour, the howls of grief, betrayal, the lewd vows
Paid to anyone who'd lick my dusty wounds—
With every word, a lie drifts into silence. The news:
God Bites Man. Blind with dust of flesh, the gore
Of an ill wind, I kneel. Silence. I need you more,

Friend, than air. Simon says, *Take up again*
Your sane semblance. Easy to obey
When the heart listens. Am I Abel or Cain
When cock's a-hoop and ta-ra-diddle rocks
The cradle? But what's enough? It's plain
Our mother's wound's a word and words decay
To dust. Or worse, her tears return to flesh
And blood runs out her man-making gash.

Graceless I fell from mother-arms; from all
That fall the tears turn into blood. The fame
Of fall is the rising from. I hear you call,
Mother of all, and feign a rise, but the name
Of one whose word's enough to make dust crawl
Upright on this hill of sorrow will come
Only to lips unsealed by the mortal kiss
Of flesh on flesh. Without that word, the abyss.

IX Sermon for the Women

Today the old man who smothered his wife
          went free. This was mercy.
Today the troops who burned in their tanks a week ago
          made a rubbery stink in the desert.
Today the infantry recruits capered
          like marionettes before the cameras.
Today a drunken senator snored
          while a woman screamed for help in his garden.
Tonight the woman from Ecuador sleeps with three children

under the freeway ramp. Her man is working nights
stacking shelves in a Miami supermarket.

Today two brokers agreed on a price;
    twelve hundred workers met in a hall and voted.
Today the editors blessed our leaders for ending
    the week's war. Sheik and emir returned
    to their desert palaces.
Today six thousand barrels of toxic sludge
    were unloaded from barges in Dakar.
Today the cop pumped thirty slugs into the heart
    of the man-shaped target, for practice.
Tonight they buried the child on the Kurdestan mountain
    while her mother soothed another's fever. Her keening
    rose higher than the blustering helicopters.

Today the deacon fingered the choirboy's anus;
    the pastor wrote out cheque after cheque
    in the presbytery.
Today the brawny oiled-up hermaphrodite posed
    and pranced before the gymnasium mirrors.
Today the greyhaired man, who knew this woman
    seven years, punched her, raped her,
        then apologised.
Today the three leaders who professed to love peace
    sat in the city of peace and continued their quarrel.
Tonight the wife read a story that could be her own.
    Her husband sat in his basement den,
    leaning back in his armchair, staring at nothing.

Tonight, a girl straightened up from the finished page.
    A deep breath. Then she leaned
    forward again into the light.
Tonight a woman felt the planets
    spin and wheel, wheel and tilt,
    and hummed their music.
Tonight you lift the child from his outcry

And hold him to your breast.
Today, these three who love peace are still
On the long pilgrimage to peace.

X Third Fall

Ach! Tastes ill, this dust, its mortal bloody tang.
Let me drop at last under my weight of wrong.
Where I am fallen, false pity's patrons raise
Memories to stay me. Rub spittle into dust, and there's
Our ancient Father, frowning from on high.
Then he takes off in a cumulus of goodbye.
Father of my own making, step light and even.
Come and go light's way, so *I will be forgiven.*

With him the women, one with her worried frown,
The other fairly smiling; she on his left in a gown
Not much in fashion; she on his right all blue hues,
Glad as forget-me-nots. Handsome the one who does,
But lovely the one who gives. Neither is prized
For personal virtues. On this grey road beside
The striding father, wife and mistress have given
All and nothing for love, so *they will be forgiven.*

Close at their heels trail Brothers, Cousins,
Sisters, Uncles, Aunts, Nuns, Jesuits, dozens
To whom I feel obliged, for the tremor of a chance
Remark or toy or joyful insult, to commence
Resentment. Swallowed anger feeds on fantasy:
Dozens of bloodless enemies are murdered savagely
And sent unshriven to doomsday terrors. They can go
Now to a hell of their own making, or accept their due
Share of these ancient pains and so, of their own volition,
Pass into peace passing all *and be forgiven.*
How much longer can this long worm possess
Me, this carcass eat itself? What of the sweats

And stinks of lust? Greed's gruels and saccharins?
Advance to play and replay a thousand scenes,
One by one: Companion, Colleague, Contestant,
Prizewinner, Egotist, Superior. Let expectant
Self take the Victim's role as you take turns to recite
How many ways I have badgered and hated you, spite
Riddling me while you gained Port Success
And my skiff drifted toward the Venereal Rocks.

Father, free me from these creatures of the seven
Sins of my own making, so *I will be forgiven.*

XI Tango Magdalena

Tears glazed her eyes, like jade beads in water—
Real tears, though they deceived—a jade mirror
Of vacant heaven. Our fevered loving would sate her,
Then repentance. Oh how this plough could furrow
Her flesh with gasps and cries! Love levelled her, terror
Invaded her to the throat—ecstasy! Later
The edgy smile, the frenzy, the clawed spasm that tore her
Even in the hour of unbidden tears, her mood borrowed
From ancient adulterous myth. Those tears accuse
And then forgive. They spill on her cheek to slake
Anguish, that relentless thirst. We began again with a kiss
to round the circle: Spring's looting tongue, Summer's ache,
Fall's bloody fruit, Winter's icy word, to use
In season, when she'll weep again for our sake.

XII Garment

Bad, friends. Angelic sidewise sidewinders have stripped
Those pretensions, those semblances you understand

As understandings: that I am man (for a moment, I crave
Your indulgence); that, as human, so divine I breathe soulfire,
Though I have let be stripped from me all that—out of desire
For the soul's nakedness—you know of me, you know me—not
As friend, nor as angel, nor as ripping wind—but as the snake
Uncoiling, whipping—whipped into surrender.

So now, the joke goes, as you know me
Without the insignia of voice, the clout of skin
Stretched on the bone drum, you want me to recover
A demeanour, some smile-mask or other, some wide-awake
Wide-open pain-mask howling for attention, for your
Forgiveness, the coil-uncoil of lying explanations
To allow you to see yourselves as friends in me
Here naked in the mirror of your forgiveness, to license
You to clothe me in your suffering,
To be Adam again for you
On your tree of shame.

XIII Ecce

Father, father, who gave
Us this deadly flesh, why
Do you not wait close
Enough to hear? Did you
Give us this pain out of love,
This death of your speechless will?
Must I now let go
This likeness of you?

Poor body, you have used
Me for the cruel dances
Of drill-sergeant and recruit,
Of drunken killer
And his hollow *daimon*.

How can I let go
Flesh and its shadow?

Poor brain, cage
Of reason, team captain, watchman,
Helpless witness to the strut
Of fame's cock-a-snoot
Half-hour to-do,
Here I let go.

Why vex me with needs
And claims? Being one
With your multitude,
I take off this worn frame
Of self, emptied
So I may let go.

Cast me as a spoonful of dust,
Echo in a wine-jar,
Voice that cries day and night
Over avenues, suburbs,
Cornfields, powerplants. Father
I cannot know, claim me,
Now I let go.

XIV Pietà

Enter the peace of the Mother of Sorrow.
Here is the womb's red silence.
Rest. Let her bear your weight.
Let her hold you in silence.

Behind, the labyrinth between lives,
The life given and the life taken.

Beyond, the dark path to the centre.
Sleep in her wise silence.

She who holds you in life and death
To her heart, the figure for love,
Cold as marble, yet no betrayal,
Offers you, her child, her life.
With your last breath, the word for love
Takes form in her unfailing silence.

XV Miserere

Dark rises through stony ground.
From the hill the city spins
And reels with its mobbed streets.
Streaks of light wheel and flow.

The world narrows to a cave.
I am found with the same shape
I was born into: the Stripped Fool.
You who are called to believe

A shadow in a cave,
Take the stir of wind
Through grass as prophecy.
Take every breath as truth.

Samarkand

Daniel, the late-born, has brought us down
To the beach on his first holiday to learn
All there is to know of gullsky, seawind.
He stretches out his hand to the Pacific,
Rigid with a deep excitement. In a while,
We track through the dunes until we find
A sheltered spot behind a drifted log.

I want to teach him sandcastles, to work
With spade and pail and patience against the way
Sand loses itself in sand. But he shovels and sifts
To no purpose, as a gull wears the wind, and soon
Tires. You put him to your breast.
He plunges to an amniotic dream.

While he's beyond my tutelage, I toil.
A wall rises to stop a valley's mouth.
Many towers on the wall; a *motte* and *fosse*;
Unnumbered loyal defenders within. For miles
The crenellated fortress rises round
The new city. Towers, domes, a piazza laid
Open before the basilica, all declare
And measure the ruler's power, so while he sleeps
He prospers. A seer foretells he'll govern
With fair heart and even hand, and be called great,
And his capitol will survive a millennium.

He opens his eyes. He smiles. He shakes himself.
On all fours, he goes to inspect his kingdom.
One knee flattens a palace. A small fist sinks
Into a terrace, a temple, a triumphal arch.
He pushes forward, breaches the great wall.
All vanishes into sand that was an empire
For the golden age you nursed him and he slept.

Sea Writer

SANDS
Sand is the history of shell and rock,
The changed world received from our forebears,
How it prevails, headland to headland, dune
To wave—*and* the gulls' mockery!

Sand has every right to arrange its own
Rhetoric, grind it as fine as it likes,
Even to mock its own definitions,
Its fame for taking time's measure with plenty left

To span a beach for the next ice age and more.
We can stand to admire it, or walk off on it.
Even its banality's worth remarking.
Come, walk with me as far as that green cliff.

Make anthologies of its gleams, the means
Glass uses to make metaphors. Its power
Will weave a silky skin around stones,
Although its cruelty may leave you blind.

You will show unlikely mastery
If you can say, precisely, fluently,
Sand, sand, sand, sand, sand.

TIDES

And you who bow to your work here and there
Under the headland, shielding your eyes with your hand
Betimes against the glare—no ancient rights attach
To your lifetime's attachment to wavelet and smooth rock,
So don't bark in your rough way, so famously 'direct',
About fishers, kelp-gatherers, driftwood-mongers.

Stay faithful to your impressions: give them purpose.
The tides that broadcast your intentions are also your
Unruly editors, your disobedient caretakers,
Always ready to clear away your inventions.
Discover a prospect, a view, and in time you will change
All we thought we knew for generations.
But we distract you. Please, carry on with your work.

WORDS

We traced these signs with stick or fingerbone
On the exhausted rock and shell to claim
No heritage, leave no memorial,
But merely to practice our sad craft, to teach
Kelp-gatherer and beachcomber how
Sand is matter, process, and *the word, a sign*
That sand is history, making none of its own,
Since the collapsing waters heave it into mere
Resemblances of greater meaning afloat
Among darker shapes in the breaking waves.

Self-Portrait, with Masks
Homage to Rembrandt

Another version of that serious boy
Tried on a frown, a leer, a cocked
Eyebrow, locked in the upstairs bathroom
With imaginary partners. He spoke
Sternly to them from the silent side
Of the brute who wrestled other brutes
In the playground to earn a tough-guy name,
Losing more than he won in any game.

Was it Onan made him vain, pale?
Ah, that stonefaced town, where they still
Think every thought's a sin and every mirror
Stares at its sinner and the stout priest
Sets absolution at a price he knows
Can't be paid. This mask is hollow-cheeked,
Lit from inside like a Halloween lantern
Hanging in Hell's darkest cavern.

Look yourself in the eye,
Though light and mirror be poor.
Take note of that stare. Take the whole
Face on its own terms, set
Like a fortress on the curve
Of shadowy shoulders—paint
Stroked and thumbed into place—
To what end? *Understand me*
(It speaks, this masked familiar),
Posterity is not my master.
Nor is blindfold Fate. Nor am I
My own creator. Pray for me.